Guide to Markdown Mode for Emacs

Jason R. Blevins

Guide to Markdown Mode for Emacs

Jason R. Blevins

ISBN 978-1978118836

Leanpub

This is a Leanpub book. Leanpub empowers authors and publishers with the Lean Publishing process. Lean Publishing is the act of publishing an in-progress ebook using lightweight tools and many iterations to get reader feedback, pivot until you have the right book and build traction once you do.

This work is licensed under a Creative Commons Attribution-NonCommercial-ShareAlike 4.0 International License

Contents

1. **Introduction** 1
   - 1.1 Quick Reference 2
   - 1.2 Markdown 4
   - 1.3 History 7
   - 1.4 Acknowledgments 8
2. **Installation & Configuration** 9
   - 2.1 Installation Methods 9
   - 2.2 Configuring Markdown 12
   - 2.3 Customization 16
3. **Movement & Editing** 19
   - 3.1 Headings 21
   - 3.2 Paragraphs 29
   - 3.3 Blockquotes 29
   - 3.4 Lists 30
   - 3.5 Paragraph & Block Movement 32
   - 3.6 Indentation 33
   - 3.7 Code Blocks 36
   - 3.8 Horizontal Rules 37
   - 3.9 Emphasis: Italic & Bold 38
   - 3.10 Inline Code 39
   - 3.11 Links & Images 40
   - 3.12 Line Breaks 44
   - 3.13 Killing Elements 45
   - 3.14 Markdown Do 45
   - 3.15 Markup Promotion & Demotion 46
   - 3.16 Markup Completion 47
   - 3.17 Markdown Maintenance Commands 47

4. Extensions ... 49

- 4.1 Fenced Code Blocks ... 49
- 4.2 Footnotes ... 54
- 4.3 Definition Lists ... 55
- 4.4 Comments ... 56
- 4.5 Task List Items (Checkboxes) ... 57
- 4.6 Subscripts and Superscripts ... 57
- 4.7 Metadata ... 58
- 4.8 Wiki Links ... 59
- 4.9 Mathematical Expressions (LaTeX) ... 61
- 4.10 GitHub Flavored Markdown (GFM) Mode ... 62

5. Previewing & Exporting Files ... 65

- 5.1 Markup Hiding ... 66
- 5.2 Compiling to a Temporary Buffer or the Kill Ring ... 67
- 5.3 Static HTML Preview ... 68
- 5.4 Static HTML Export & View ... 68
- 5.5 Live Preview Mode ... 69
- 5.6 Opening in a Standalone Markdown Previewer ... 70
- 5.7 Preview & Export Customization ... 71

6. Tips ... 73

- 6.1 Using Markdown Mode with Other File Extensions ... 73
- 6.2 Switching and Toggling Markup ... 74
- 6.3 Linking to or Including Custom CSS ... 74
- 6.4 Imenu and Imenu-List ... 76
- 6.5 File Local Variables ... 79
- 6.6 Generating a Table of Contents ... 80
- 6.7 Highlighting and Preserving Whitespace ... 82
- 6.8 Using Flyspell with Markdown Mode ... 82
- 6.9 Keeping Notes in a Local Wiki ... 83
- 6.10 Integration with Deft Mode ... 84
- 6.11 MathJax Integration ... 85
- 6.12 Using Pre- and Post-Processors ... 86
- 6.13 Using a Custom Web Browser ... 87
- 6.14 Using Marked 2 as a Standalone Previewer ... 89
- 6.15 Pandoc Mode ... 90
- 6.16 R Markdown ... 91

	6.17	Tracking Changes with CriticMarkup Mode	92
	6.18	Editing HTML as Markdown	93
	6.19	Editing Markdown Tables with Org Table Mode	94
7.	**Markdown Mode Development**		97
	7.1	Testing the Development Version	97
	7.2	Reporting Bugs and Issues	98
	7.3	Submitting Patches or GitHub Pull Requests	98
8.	**Conclusion**		101
	8.1	Looking Back and Looking Ahead	101
	8.2	Further Reading	101

1. Introduction

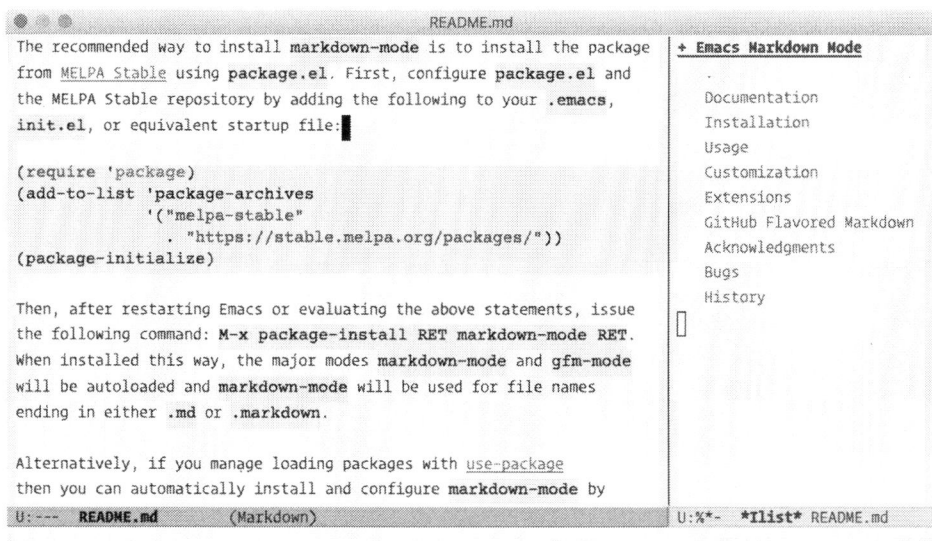

Markdown Mode Screenshot

This *Guide* describes how to install, use, and customize Markdown Mode, a major mode for editing Markdown-formatted text files in Emacs. It is not intended to be a replacement for the online manual, but rather to supplement and extend the manual for users who want to learn to use Markdown Mode more effectively.

The goal of this book is to make writing and publishing with Markdown in Emacs more enjoyable and efficient. The hope is that through examples and detailed descriptions of the various commands and customizable variables, users can learn more about Emacs itself and also improve their Markdown writing workflows.

This book covers the usual basic information about obtaining, installing and configuring Markdown Mode, but it also addresses advanced usage such as subtree and structure editing, defun and page movement, marking, narrowing, region manipulation, etc. It goes beyond the basic documentation by also discussing interaction with other packages and systems such as Flyspell mode, CriticMarkup mode, Pandoc mode, Deft, HTML as Markdown mode, and MathJax. Finally, it also contains tips and tricks for custom configuration options such as custom CSS stylesheets, using pre- and post-processors, customizing faces, keeping notes in a local wiki, etc.

This guide is based on **Markdown Mode version** 2.3. Markdown Mode and this guide were written by Jason Blevins. Markdown Mode is free software, licensed under the GNU General Public License (GPL) version 3 or later, and it may be freely obtained from the Markdown Mode homepage.

1.1 Quick Reference

If you are a seasoned Markdown Mode user, here is a quick reference table including new version 2.3 features:

Action	Keybinding
Headings	
Insert heading depending on context	C-c C-s h
Insert heading, prefer setext	C-c C-s H
Insert atx heading of level # = 1, 2, ... 6	C-c C-s #
Insert setext heading of level 1	C-c C-s !
Insert setext heading of level 2	C-c C-s @
Inline Elements	
Bold	C-c C-s b
Italics	C-c C-s i
Inline code	C-c C-s c
kbd tag	C-c C-s k
Wiki link	C-c C-s w
Block Elements	
Preformatted/code block	C-c C-s p
Preformatted/code block (region)	C-c C-s P
Blockquote	C-c C-s q
Blockquote (region)	C-c C-s Q
GFM code block	C-c C-s C
Edit code block in indirect buffer	C-c '
Links and Images	
Insert or edit link (inline, reference, or URL)	C-c C-l
Insert or edit image (inline or reference)	C-c C-i
Follow link at point	C-c C-o
Jump between reference link and definition	C-c C-d
Move to next link	M-n
Move to previous link	M-p
Footnotes	

Action	Keybinding
Insert footnote	`C-c C-s f`
Jump between footnote and definition	`C-c C-d`
List Items & List Editing	
Insert new list item (same level)	`M-RET`
Insert new list item (same level)	`C-c C-j`
Insert new list item (parent level)	`C-u C-c C-j`
Insert new list item (child level)	`C-u C-u C-c C-j`
Move list item up	`C-c <up>`
Move list item down	`C-c <down>`
Outdent/promote list item	`C-c <left>`
Indent/demote list item	`C-c <right>`
Toggle GFM checkbox	`C-c C-x C-x`
Horizontal Rules	
Insert default horizontal rule string	`C-c C-s -`
Killing and Yanking	
Kill element and keep text in kill ring	`C-c C-k`
Yank text back into buffer	`C-y`
Movement by Paragraph	
Backward paragraph	`M-{`
Forward paragraph	`M-}`
Mark paragraph	`M-h`
Movement by Block	
Backward block	`C-M-{`
Forward block	`C-M-}`
Mark block	`C-c M-h`
Narrow to block	`C-x n b`
Widen	`C-x n w`
Movement by Section (Defun)	
Beginning of section	`C-M-a`
End of section	`C-M-e`
Mark section	`C-M-h`
Mark subtree	`C-c C-M-h`
Narrow to section	`C-x n d`
Narrow to subtree	`C-x n s`
Widen	`C-x n w`
Outline & List Movement	
Next heading or list item	`C-c C-n`
Previous heading or list item	`C-c C-p`
Next heading or list item (same level)	`C-c C-f`
Previous heading or list item (same level)	`C-c C-b`
Move up to parent heading or list item	`C-c C-u`

Action	Keybinding
Outline Visibility Cycling	
Cycle visibility globally	`S-TAB`
Cycle visibility of heading at point	`TAB`
Outline Subtree Editing	
Move subtree up	`C-c <up>`
Move subtree down	`C-c <down>`
Promote subtree	`C-c <left>`
Demote subtree	`C-c <right>`
Region Editing	
Indent region	`C-c >`
Exdent region	`C-c <`
Promotion and Demotion	
Promote element at point	`C-c -`
Demote element at point	`C-c =`
Markup Completion	
Complete markup at point or in region	`C-c C-]`
Complete markup in buffer	`C-c C-c ]`
Markdown & Utility Commands	
Run Markdown, output to temporary buffer	`C-c C-c m`
Run Markdown, export to file	`C-c C-c e`
Run Markdown, preview in browser	`C-c C-c p`
Run Markdown, export, and preview	`C-c C-c v`
Run Markdown, save to kill ring	`C-c C-c w`
Toggle live preview mode	`C-c C-c l`
Open external previewer	`C-c C-c o`
Check references in buffer	`C-c C-c c`
Renumber ordered lists in buffer	`C-c C-c n`
Toggles and Settings	
Toggle markup hiding	`C-c C-x C-m`
Toggle URL hiding	`C-c C-x C-l`
Toggle native code block font lock	`C-c C-x C-f`
Toggle inline images	`C-c C-x C-i`
Toggle LaTeX math support	`C-c C-x C-e`
Toggle GFM checkbox	`C-c C-x C-x`

1.2 Markdown

Markdown is a lightweight markup language, originally created by John Gruber in late 2003 and released in 2004. Markdown aims to be simultaneously easy to write and easy to read.

It takes many cues from previous, similar attempts such as atx, by Aaron Swartz,[1] setext, by Ian Feldman, and Textile, by Dean Allen, as well as from existing conventions for marking up plain text email.

"Markdown" is also used to refer to the original Markdown processor, also written by John Gruber, which is a Perl script that converts plain Markdown-formatted text input to HTML output. It is distributed under a BSD-style license and is included with, or available as a plugin for, several content management systems. In the remainder I will refer to the processor by its filename, Markdown.pl, to distinguish between the Markdown syntax and the Perl script. After the original Perl implementation, Markdown processors have been implemented by others in a variety of programming languages. Some examples are, in no particular order, PHP Markdown Extra, Python Markdown, MultiMarkdown (Perl and C), Pandoc (Haskell), Discount (C), Maruku (Ruby), RedCarpet (Ruby), Kramdown (Ruby), Showdown (JavaScript), and CommonMark (C and JavaScript).

Markdown Syntax Reference

For reference, below is a plain-text summary of Markdown's syntax. Additional details about each type of element are explained in the course of describing the Markdown Mode editing commands. See the original Markdown syntax page for complete details.

```
# First-Level Header

## Second-Level Header

### Third-Level header

Paragraphs are separated by a blank line.

Text styles: _italic_, *italic*, __bold__, **bold**, `code`.

Horizontal rules:

---

***
```

---

[1] John Gruber described Aaron Swartz as his "muse" while developing Markdown, due to his early enthusiasm for and feedback on the project. Aaron Swartz also wrote html2text, a popular HTML to Markdown converter written in Python.

```
Unordered list:

    * red
    * yellow
    * blue

Ordered list:

    1. apples
    2. oranges
    3. pears

Inline [link](https://jblevins.org/).

![Image alt text](emacs.svg)

Reference [link][tag].

[tag]: https://jblevins.org/

Implicit reference [link][].

[link]: https://jblevins.org/projects/markdown-mode/
```

Characters can be backslash-escaped in Markdown. That is, characters which are ordinarily interpreted by Markdown as formatting commands will instead be interpreted literally if preceded by a backslash. For example, when you need to type a literal asterisk or underscore:

```
This is *italic*, but this \*is not\*.
```

Markdown.pl also does not transform any text within raw block-level HTML elements (although some other processors do). Thus it is possible to include sections of HTML within a Markdown source document by wrapping them in block-level HTML tags. However, with a small number of exceptions (e.g., comments and `kbd` tags) Markdown Mode does not explicitly support inline HTML.

Additional Information

For additional information on Markdown syntax, you can refer to the following links:

- Markdown Syntax - Original syntax description by John Gruber
- Markdown Dingus - Online converter using Markdown.pl
- Babelmark 2 - Online converter comparing many Markdown processors
- Wikipedia article - Background information on Markdown with syntax examples
- Mastering Markdown - Guide to Markdown and extensions by GitHub
- Pandoc User's Guide - Markdown and Pandoc extensions
- PHP Markdown Reference - Markdown and PHP Markdown Extra extensions
- Write better Markdown - Style guide by Brett Terpstra

1.3 History

Markdown Mode was originally written and is still maintained by Jason Blevins. The initial release, version 1.1, was created on May 24, 2007. As of this writing, the latest stable version of Markdown Mode is version 2.3, released on August 31, 2017. For a complete list of changes, see the version 2.3 release notes or those for previous versions:

- 2017-05-26: Version 2.2
- 2016-01-09: Version 2.1
- 2013-03-24: Version 2.0
- 2013-01-25: Version 1.9
- 2011-08-15: Version 1.8.1
- 2011-08-12: Version 1.8
- 2009-10-01: Version 1.7
- 2008-06-04: Version 1.6
- 2007-10-11: Version 1.5
- 2007-06-29: Version 1.4
- 2007-06-05: Version 1.3
- 2007-05-25: Version 1.2
- 2007-05-24: Version 1.1

Historically, version numbering began at 1.1 because the source code was originally stored in RCS (Revision Control System), which numbers revisions starting at 1.1 by default. After version 1.5, the source was moved to Git, where it still resides today. See the chapter on Markdown Mode Development for instructions on how to obtain the source code.

1.4 Acknowledgments

Markdown Mode has benefited greatly from the efforts of the many volunteers who have sent patches, test cases, bug reports, suggestions, helped with packaging, etc. Thank you for your contributions! Markdown Mode is much more robust and includes many additional features as a result of your efforts. Below is a partial list of contributors (in alphabetical order). See the GitHub contributors graph and the commit log for more details.

Masayuki Ataka, Hilko Bengen, Jonas Bernoulli, Greg Bognar, Roger Bolsius, Daniel Brotsky, Cyril Brulebois, Daniel Burrows, Donald Ephraim Curtis, Julien Danjou, Werner Dittmann, Jeremiah Dodds, Carsten Dominik, Michael Dwyer, Dmitry Dzhus, Peter Eisentraut, Conal Elliott, Bryan Fink, Gunnar Franke, Samuel Freilich, Shigeru Fukaya, Peter S. Galbraith, Francois Gannaz, David Glasser, Matus Goljer, Kévin Le Gouguec, Marijn Haverbeke, Isaac Hodes, Philippe Ivaldi, Zhenlei Jia, Peter Jones, Antonis Kanouras, Marcin Kasperski, Keshav Kini, Dave Kleinschmidt, Vasily Korytov, Joost Kremers, Bryan Kyle, Kévin Le Gouguec, Chris Lott, Christopher J. Madsen, Tom May, Danny McClanahan, Matt McClure, Howard Melman, Eric Merritt, Nelson Minar, Stefan Monnier, Makoto Motohashi, Jon Mountjoy, Akinori Musha, Pierre Neidhardt, Spanti Nicola, Theresa O'Connor, George Ogata, Paul W. Rankin, Jose A. Ortega Ruiz, Max Penet, Nicolas Petton, Jorge Israel Peña, Scott Pfister, Kevin Porter, Steve Purcell, Alec Resnick, Christophe Rhodes, Enrico Scholz, Dale Sedivec, Ankit Solanki, Tyler Smith, Michael Sperber, Mike Sperber, Vitalie Spinu, Philipp Stephani, Moogen Tian, Vegard Vesterheim, Tim Visher, Ben Voui, Sebastian Wiesner, Peter Williams, Tianxiang Xiong, Ian Yang, Syohei Yoshida, and Google, Inc.

* * *

2. Installation & Configuration

There are many ways to load packages in Emacs, and the following three are covered in this section: installation using the built-in Emacs package manager (recommended), installation using a system-wide package manager, and manual installation.

Markdown Mode is compatible with Emacs 24.3 and later, and it has few dependencies. To preview files and export to HTML, you will need to install and configure a Markdown processor (e.g., Markdown.pl). Also, to enable editing of code blocks in indirect buffers using `C-c '` (`markdown-edit-code-block`), you will need to install the `edit-indirect` package.

 This chapter covers installing the stable version of Markdown Mode, but installing the development version is similar. If you would like to test the development version see the Markdown Mode Development chapter at the end.

2.1 Installation Methods

Emacs Package Manager

The recommended way to install Markdown Mode is to use the built-in Emacs package manager, `package.el`, which has been included in Emacs since version 23. Markdown Mode can be installed via the `markdown-mode` package in the MELPA Stable repository.[1]

First, you will need to configure the package manager to use the MELPA Stable repository by adding the following to your `.emacs`, `init.el`, or equivalent init file:

---

[1] MELPA is Milkypostman's Emacs Lisp Package Archive at http://melpa.org/.

```
(require 'package)
(add-to-list 'package-archives
    '("melpa-stable" . "https://stable.melpa.org/packages/"))
(package-initialize)
```

Then, after restarting Emacs or evaluating the above statements, issue the following command: `M-x package-install RET markdown-mode`. When installing this way, the major modes `markdown-mode` and `gfm-mode` will be autoloaded and `markdown-mode` will be invoked automatically for file names ending in either `.md` or `.markdown`.[2]

Alternatively, if you manage loading packages with use-package (a practice I highly recommend) then you can automatically install and configure `markdown-mode` by adding a declaration such as the one below to your init file (this is an example, so adjust the settings as needed):

```
(use-package markdown-mode
  :ensure t
  :commands (markdown-mode gfm-mode)
  :mode (("README\\.md\\'" . gfm-mode))
  :init (setq markdown-command "/usr/local/bin/multimarkdown"))
```

OS Package Manager

Markdown Mode is also available in various package managers on several operating systems. You should confirm that the package you install contains the latest stable version (and please notify the package maintainer if not). These packages also typically do not byte compile the source files or configure them to load automatically, so you may still need to follow the Manual Installation instructions in the next section.

MacOS: MacOS users who use Homebrew can install the markdown-mode formula, which in turn obtains the latest stable version of Markdown Mode from GitHub.

```
brew tap dunn/emacs
brew install dunn/emacs/markdown-mode
```

---

[2] See the tip on Using Markdown Mode with Other File Extensions for instructions on how to configure Emacs to use `markdown-mode` for file extensions other than `.md` and `.markdown`.

This will install files in /usr/local/share/emacs/site-lisp/markdown-mode. Depending on where you obtained Emacs, this directory may or may not be in your load-path, so you may need to add it as described in the Manual Installation section that follows.

 If you are a MacPorts user, unfortunately there does not seem to be an up-to-date port. The existing markdown-mode.el port currently points to a Git revision from 2014. There is also a pending ticket for a new port, but there has been no activity. Rather than installing from MacPorts, I recommend using the Emacs package manager as described above.

Debian and Ubuntu Linux: On Debian-based distributions, Markdown Mode can be installed via the elpa-markdown-mode package.

```
sudo apt-get install elpa-markdown-mode
```

FreeBSD: FreeBSD users can install the textproc/markdown-mode.el port, but note that the installed files are not byte compiled. Users who install this port will also need to edit their init files following the Manual Installation instructions in the next section to load Markdown Mode.

NetBSD: Markdown Mode is available in pkgsrc as textproc/markdown-mode, but (as of May 8, 2017) it installs and byte-compiles an outdated version of Markdown Mode. If you use this package, you will also need to edit your init file following the Manual Installation instructions below, to load Markdown Mode. Rather than installing this package, use the Emacs package manager as described above.

```
pkg_add textproc/markdown-mode
```

Manual Installation

Alternatively, you can manually download and install Markdown Mode. First, download the latest stable version[3] and save the file where Emacs can find it (i.e., a directory in your load-path). You can then configure markdown-mode and gfm-mode to load automatically by adding the following to your init file:

---

[3]The latest stable version is available at https://jblevins.org/projects/markdown-mode/markdown-mode.el.

```
(autoload 'markdown-mode "markdown-mode"
   "Major mode for editing Markdown files" t)
(add-to-list 'auto-mode-alist '("\\.markdown\\'" . markdown-mode))
(add-to-list 'auto-mode-alist '("\\.md\\'" . markdown-mode))

(autoload 'gfm-mode "markdown-mode"
    "Major mode for GitHub Flavored Markdown files" t)
(add-to-list 'auto-mode-alist '("README\\.md\\'" . gfm-mode))
```

2.2 Configuring Markdown

Although strictly speaking no configuration is *necessary*, there are a few settings that most users will want to customize. The most important of these is the `markdown-command` variable, which tells Markdown Mode where to find an external program on your system for converting Markdown to HTML. You should customize this variable so that Markdown Mode uses your Markdown processor of choice.

`markdown-command`

    String, default: `"markdown"`.

    The command used to convert Markdown to HTML, along with any necessary command-line options. The default is to look for an executable named `markdown` in the Emacs `exec-path`.

If you are using the customize interface, you simply need to type the path to your Markdown script or binary in the "Markdown Command" field in the customize interface (e.g., `/usr/local/bin/multimarkdown`). If you know the name of the executable, say `multimarkdown`, but you are not sure where it is located, and you are using macOS or Linux, you can find it by typing `which multimarkdown` at the command line.

To set this variable in your init file, add a line such as the following:

```
(setq markdown-command "/usr/local/bin/multimarkdown")
```

Configuring Markdown on macOS with Homebrew

If you use Homebrew, then you can install Markdown.pl, Pandoc, or MultiMarkdown by issuing one of the following commands:

```
brew install markdown
brew install pandoc
brew install multimarkdown
```

Then, in Emacs, type `M-x customize-mode RET markdown-mode` and set "Markdown Command" to the path of the executable you just installed: `/usr/local/bin/markdown`, `/usr/local/bin/pandoc`, or `/usr/local/bin/multimarkdown`.

Configuring Markdown on Windows

On Windows, you will need to use the full path including the drive letter. For example, if you installed Pandoc in `C:\Utils\Console`, then you would set `markdown-command` like this:

```
(setq markdown-command "c:/Utils/Console/pandoc.exe")
```

If you need to run Markdown as a script, with an interpreter, then you will need to add that as well. For example, to use Markdown.pl with Perl (both need to be installed), something like this should suffice:

```
(setq markdown-command "c:/path/to/perl.exe c:/path/to/Markdown.pl")
```

Passing Command Line Options to Markdown

You can also customize this variable to pass any necessary command line options to your Markdown processor. For example, to ask MultiMarkdown to enable smart typography and footnotes, you can define `markdown-command` as follows:

```
(setq markdown-command "/usr/local/bin/multimarkdown --smart --notes")
```

If you use Pandoc, you may want to configure it as follows:

```
(setq markdown-command
      (concat
       "/usr/local/bin/pandoc"
       " --from=markdown --to=html"
       " --standalone --mathjax --highlight-style=pygments"))
```

The command-line arguments ask Pandoc to convert Markdown to HTML, to produce a standalone HTML document rather than a snippet, to enable MathJax (to render LaTeX as MathML), and to use Pygments for syntax highlighting of code blocks.

Passing a File Name to Markdown

By default, Markdown Mode assumes that your Markdown processor accepts input via the standard input, or `stdin`. That is, it assumes that if you were using it from the command line, you could *pipe* input to it like so:

```
cat document.md | markdown
```

If your Markdown processor needs to be passed a file name, you will need to set another variable: `markdown-command-needs-filename`. When this variable is `nil` (the default), Markdown Mode will pass the Markdown content to `markdown-command` using `stdin`. When set to `t`, Markdown Mode will pass the name of the file as the final command line argument to `markdown-command`. Note that in the latter case, you will only be able to run `markdown-command` from buffers which are visiting a file.

> **`markdown-command-needs-filename`**
> Boolean, default: `nil`.
>
> Set to `t` if the program specified as `markdown-command` needs the filename to be specified as a command line argument, rather than reading the content from the standard input (`stdin`).

Markdown Command and `exec-path`

You can set `markdown-command` to be the full path to the executable, as in previous examples, but a better solution is to set your `exec-path` properly so that Emacs can find it without the full path. You can check this in two ways. First, to see the value of `exec-path`, issue M-x describe-variable RET exec-path. If you see the directory containing your Markdown executable in the path, then the name of the program by itself should suffice without the path (e.g., multimarkdown).

Second, you can also use the executable-find command to see if Emacs can find your Markdown processor. This isn't an interactive command, but you can run it using eval-expression via M-:. For example, to check whether Emacs can find an executable named pandoc, you can issue M-: (executable-find "pandoc"). The return value will be displayed in the minibuffer. If you see the path to pandoc, then Emacs can find it. If you see nil, then pandoc could not be found in your exec-path.

 If you attempt to preview or export your buffer and you see an error regarding the markdown command (which is the default value of the markdown-command variable), then most likely you need to check your markdown-command setting or install a Markdown processor (or both). Below are some common error messages that indicate that either the markdown binary cannot be found or markdown-command should be customized to your system:

/bin/bash: markdown: command not found

zsh:1: command not found: markdown

'markdown' is not recognized as an internal or external
    command, operable program or batch file.

 If you are having trouble setting your exec-path, a simple way to configure it is to install the exec-path-from-shell package. Its purpose is to ensure that environment variables in Emacs are the same as in your shell. This allows Emacs to find any commands you can also execute from the command line without specifying the full path.

2.3 Customization

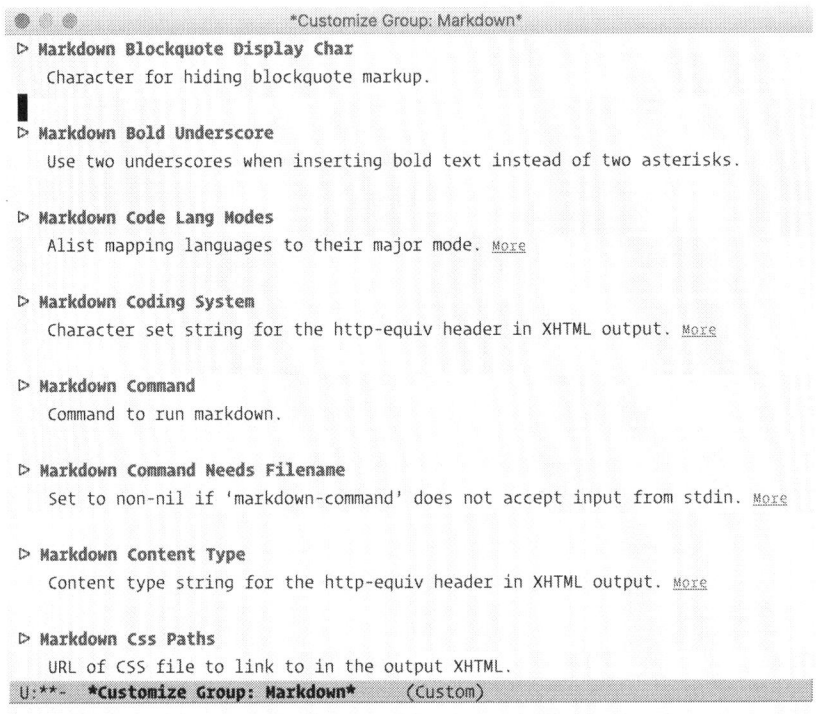

Markdown Customize Group

When in Markdown Mode, the M-x customize-mode command provides an interface to all of the available customizations. If you are using a different mode, then you will need to be more specific: M-x customize-mode RET markdown-mode. Alternatively, you can customize variables using M-x customize-group RET markdown (i.e., by customizing the *group* rather than the *mode*).

 If you use this built-in customize interface, be sure to save your changes before closing the buffer by clicking the "Apply and Save" button.

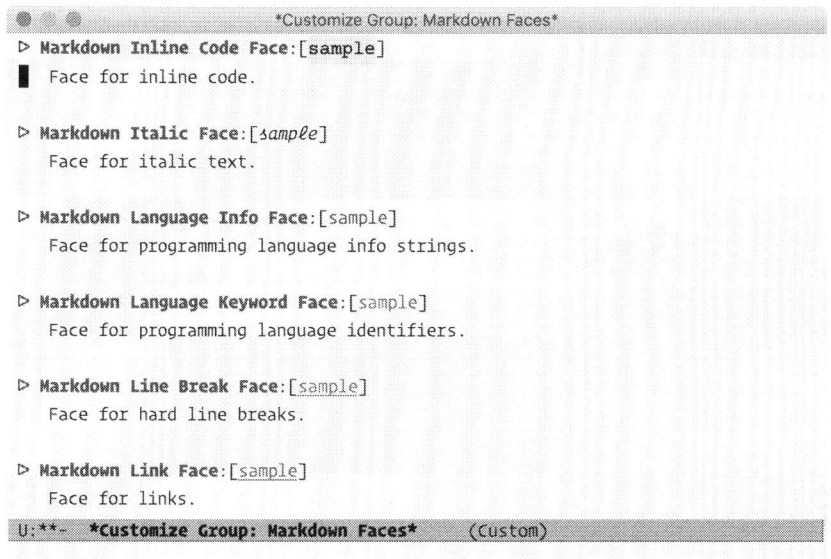

Markdown Faces Customize Group

Additionally, the faces used for font lock (syntax highlighting) can be modified to your liking—the font family, color, size, and so on—by issuing `M-x customize-group RET markdown-faces` or by using the "Markdown Faces" link at the bottom of the mode customization screen.

*   *   *

3. Movement & Editing

This section describes the movement, insertion, and editing commands provided by Markdown Mode. Commands pertaining to block elements are described first: headings, paragraphs, blockquotes, lists, code blocks, and horizontal rules. Then, commands for editing span elements are described: emphasis, code, links, images, and comments. Finally, miscellaneous editing commands are described for markup completion, markup cycling, indentation, etc. Extensions, such as footnotes, fenced code blocks, wiki links, definition lists, and checkboxes are described in the Extensions chapter that follows.

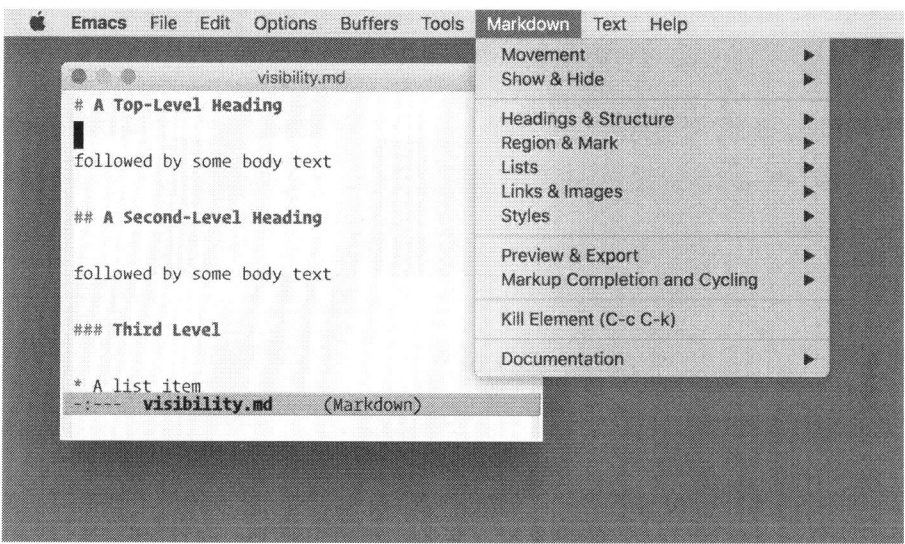

Markdown Menu in Emacs on macOS

Markdown Mode keybindings are grouped by prefixes based on their function. Like other major modes, most commands begin with C-c, the mode-specific-command-prefix. Commands are then grouped by category under a second-level prefix. For example, the commands for styling text are grouped under C-c C-s (markdown-mode-style-map). Similarly, commands for running Markdown and performing maintenance tasks reside under C-c C-c (markdown-mode-command-map). Movement and shifting commands tend to be associated with paired delimiters such as M-{ and M-} or C-c < and C-c >. If you have menu-bar-mode on, you can also access these commands from the Markdown menu.

We begin with a summary of Markdown Mode prefixes and mnemonics. The commands in each group will be described in detail below. You can obtain a list of all keybindings by pressing `C-c C-h` or `C-h m`. To see commands under a specific prefix, add `C-h` to the end of the prefix. For example, press `C-c C-s C-h` to list all commands under `C-c C-s`.

Prefix	Function
C-c C-s	Styles
C-c C-l	Links
C-c C-i	Images
C-c C-c	Commands
C-c C-x	Toggles

When you use the `C-c C-s` or `C-c C-c` prefixes, prompts will appear in the minibuffer that provide hints for a few of the most commonly used commands. You can control this by setting `markdown-enable-prefix-prompts`.

`markdown-enable-prefix-prompts`
    Boolean, default: `t`.

    When non-`nil`, display prompts when certain prefix keys are pressed. Set to `nil` to disable these prompts.

 There are several Emacs packages for providing keybinding hints, such as `which-key` and `guide-key`. If you use one of these, you can disable Markdown Mode's prefix prompts by setting `markdown-enable-prefix-prompts` to `nil`.

The following sections describe many commands for inserting markup—for headings, blockquotes, lists, source code, and so on—and many of these commands behave differently depending on whether `transient-mark-mode` is enabled or not. When it makes sense, if `transient-mark-mode` is on and there is an active region, the command applies to the text in the region. For example, `C-c C-s b` (`markdown-insert-bold`) would make the region bold. When `transient-mark-mode` is off or there is no active region, many commands then proceed to work with either the word at the point (e.g., for italics) or the current line (e.g., for headings).

There are also some parallel commands that act specifically on the region, even when `transient-mark-mode` is disabled. These commands have the same keybindings as their standard counterparts but use an uppercase letter instead. For example, `markdown-insert-blockquote` is bound to `C-c C-s q` while `markdown-blockquote-region` is bound to `C-c C-s Q`. The latter *always* applies to the region while the former only acts on the region when `transient-mark-mode` is on and the region is active.

 For users who prefer to work *without* `transient-mark-mode`, conveniently since Emacs 22 it can be enabled temporarily by pressing `C-SPC C-SPC`.

3.1 Headings

Headings in Markdown can be defined using either of two formats: atx and setext.

Atx-style headings are lines beginning with one to six hash marks (#) followed by the heading text. The number of hash marks corresponds to the level of the heading, with one being the most prominent and six being the least prominent (corresponding to the six levels of headings in HTML, <h1> through <h6>). The heading text may optionally be followed by an equal number of hash marks.

```
# First-level heading #

First section text.  Here we close the heading with a hash mark.

## Second-level heading

Second section text.  No closing hash marks here.

### Third-level heading ###

Third section text.
```

The second type of headings supported in Markdown are called setext headings, for which only two levels are defined. Instead of being surrounded by hash marks, equals signs (=) and hyphens (-) are used to underline the heading text.

```
First-level heading
===================

Second-level heading
--------------------
```

Inserting & Replacing Headings

There are two options for inserting or replacing headings: you can either insert a heading of a specific level and type or let Markdown Mode determine the level and type for you. To insert a heading of a specific level directly, simply use `C-c C-s #` where # is a number 1 through 6 (`markdown-insert-header-atx-1`, ..., `markdown-insert-header-atx-6`).

To insert setext headings directly, use `C-c C-s !` (`markdown-insert-header-setext-1`) for level one or `C-c C-s @` (`markdown-insert-header-setext-2`) for level two. Noting that ! is S-1 and @ is S-2 may make these commands easier to remember.

For automatic heading insertion use `C-c C-s h` (`markdown-insert-header-dwim`). The type and level are determined based on the previous heading. By default, the new heading will be a sibling (same level). A `C-u` prefix can be added to insert a heading that is *promoted* (lower number) by one level or a `C-u C-u` prefix can be given to insert a heading that is *demoted* (higher number) by one level.

Suppose you are currently writing in a level-two section, as in the following example, where ▌ indicates the point:

```
## Heading ##

Body text.
▌
```

Pressing `C-c C-s h`, for automatic heading insertion, creates a new level-two sibling heading:

```
## Heading ##

Body text.

## ▌##
```

Using the universal prefix, as in `C-u C-c C-s h`, creates a new level-one parent heading:

```
# ▌#
```

Using the universal prefix twice, as in `C-u C-u C-c C-s h`, creates a new level-three child heading instead:

```
### ▌###
```

To automatically insert setext-style headings, use `C-c C-s H` (`markdown-insert-header-setext-dwim`). This command behaves like `C-c C-c h` (`markdown-insert-header-dwim`) in that the level is calculated automatically and it can accept the same prefix arguments, but it uses setext (underlined) headings for levels one and two.

As with several other markup commands, if the region is active and `transient-mark-mode` is on, the heading insertion commands use the text in the region as the heading text. Next, if the current line is not blank, they use the text on the current line. Otherwise, the user is prompted to provide the heading text.

If the point is at a heading, these commands will replace the existing markup in order to update the level or type of the heading. This is useful, for example, when the automatically-determined heading level is not what you wanted: the heading level can be quickly changed as needed.

 Suppose you mistakenly insert a level-two heading and want to replace it, as in the following example:

`## Heading`▇`##`

Pressing `C-c C-s 1` replaces the heading with a level-one heading:

`# Heading`▇`#`

To remove the markup of the heading at the point, you can press `C-c C-k` (`markdown-kill-thing-at-point`) to kill the heading and add the text to the kill ring. Press `C-y` to yank the heading text back into the buffer.

 Markdown.pl and several other processors allow one to omit the whitespace between the hash mark and the heading text, but some processors and specifications such as CommonMark do require the whitespace. To help guarantee compatibility, Markdown Mode also requires whitespace. This has other advantages, for example, it allows one to use #hashtags that might wrap to the beginning of the line.

 If the length of the underline characters is not exactly right, Markdown Mode can help keep things tidy by "completing" the markup for you after the fact. See the Markup Completion section of this chapter for more details.

Outline Navigation

Markdown Mode defines keys for hierarchical navigation in headings and lists. When the point is in a list, they move between list items. Otherwise, they move between headings.

- Use `C-c C-n` and `C-c C-p` (`markdown-outline-previous` and `markdown-outline-next`) to move to the next and previous visible headings or list items *of any level*.

- Similarly, C-c C-f and C-c C-b (markdown-outline-previous-same-level and markdown-outline-next-same-level) move to the next and previous visible headings or list items *at the same level* as the one at the point.
- Finally, C-c C-u (markdown-outline-up) will move up to the parent heading or list item.

 The outline navigation commands in markdown-mode (C-c C-n, C-c C-p, C-c C-f, C-c C-b, and C-c C-u) are the same as in org-mode, which are in turn based on those in outline-minor-mode.

Movement by Defun

The usual Emacs commands can be used to move by defuns (top-level major definitions), but in Markdown Mode, **a defun is a section**. As usual, C-M-a (beginning-of-defun) will move the point to the beginning of the current or preceding defun, C-M-e (end-of-defun) will move to the end of the current or following defun, and C-M-h (mark-defun) will mark the current defun. To narrow the buffer to show only the current section, use C-x n d (narrow-to-defun) and to widen again, use C-x n w (widen) as usual.

 Defuns in Emacs are major top-level definitions. The name derives from the Emacs Lisp defun macro for defining functions. The defun movement and marking commands in Markdown Mode (C-M-a, C-M-e, and C-M-h) are the same as in Emacs more generally. Since Markdown has no functions, Markdown Mode considers section headings to be defuns.

To include the complete subtree (including any subsections) when marking and narrowing, Markdown Mode also defines C-c C-M-h (markdown-mark-subtree) and C-x n s (markdown-narrow-to-subtree).

Movement by Page

Markdown Mode also re-defines the "page" movement and marking commands in Emacs, since they aren't otherwise useful in Markdown documents. Elsewhere in Emacs, pages are defined by a regular expression given in the page-delimiter variable, usually ^L (control-L, the page break control code). Markdown Mode redefines a page to be a complete top-level subtree, so you can navigate between top-level headings using the standard Emacs page movement keys: `C-x [` and `C-x ]` (`markdown-backward-page` and `markdown-forward-page`). To mark the current top-level subtree, use `C-x C-p` (`markdown-mark-page`). To narrow the buffer to show only the current top-level subtree, use `C-x n p` (`markdown-narrow-to-page`) and to widen again, use `C-x n w` (`widen`) as usual.

Visibility Cycling

Markdown Mode supports `org-mode`-style visibility cycling for headings and sections. There are two types of visibility cycling: global and local.

Pressing `S-TAB` (`markdown-shifttab`) cycles *globally* between three levels of visibility, as shown in the screenshot below:

1. headings only (overview),
2. top-level headings only (contents),
3. all sections visible (show all).

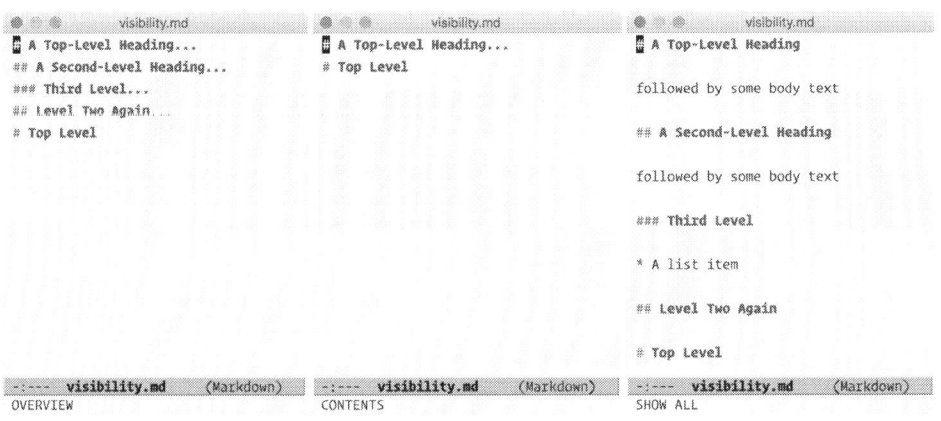

Global Visibility Cycling

On the other hand, pressing `TAB` (`markdown-cycle`) while the point is at a heading will cycle through three levels of visibility *locally* for the current subtree:

1. all subsections and sub-headings completely folded,
2. child headings visible,
3. all subsections and sub-headings fully visible.

Subtree Editing

Entire subtrees of ATX headings can be promoted and demoted with C-c <left> and C-c <right> (markdown-promote and markdown-demote). Conveniently, these are the same keybindings used for promotion and demotion of list items. If the point is at a list item, they operate on the list item. Otherwise, they operate on the current heading subtree. Similarly, subtrees can be moved up and down with C-c <up> and C-c <down> (markdown-move-up and markdown-move-down).

 These commands are based on functions from outline.el that are regular-expression-based, and so they currently do not work properly if there are setext headings in the region.

Note the following "boundary" behavior for promotion and demotion. Any level-six headings will not be demoted further (i.e., they remain at level six, since Markdown and HTML do not define more than six levels of headings) and any level-one headings will be promoted away entirely (i.e., the heading markup will be removed, since level-zero headings are undefined).

Heading Customization

Markdown Mode distinguishes between *symmetric* and *asymmetric* atx heading markup. Symmetric headings have an equal number of hash marks at the beginning and end of the line. Asymmetric headings have only leading hash marks. Both are valid, so this is an aesthetic choice. You can customize Markdown Mode to fit your preference by setting the markdown-asymmetric-header variable.

markdown-asymmetric-header
> nil or t, default: nil.
>
> Determines if atx heading style will be asymmetric.
>
> When nil, balanced markup will be inserted at the beginning and end of the line around the heading title.
>
> ## Heading ##
>
> Set to a non-nil value to use asymmetric heading styling, placing heading markup only at the beginning of the line.

```
## Heading
```

Example:

```
(setq markdown-asymmetric-header t)
```

Markdown Mode also has the ability to scale the font sizes used for headings in proportion to their importance (as in AUCTeX, for instance). To enable this, customize `markdown-header-scaling` or set it in your init file.

`markdown-header-scaling`
    Boolean, default: `nil`.

    Determines whether Markdown Mode uses different font sizes for headings of different levels. Set to a non-`nil` value to inherit from the `variable-pitch` for headings with font sizes that correspond to the scaling factors in the `markdown-header-scaling-values` list.

`markdown-header-scaling-values`
    List of floats, default: `(2.0 1.7 1.4 1.1 1.0 1.0)`.

    List of six scaling values, relative to baseline, to use for headings of levels one through six. Only used when `markdown-header-scaling` is non-`nil`.

For finer control over the heading faces, Markdown Mode defines separate heading faces for each heading level:

```
markdown-header-face-1      markdown-header-face-4
markdown-header-face-2      markdown-header-face-5
markdown-header-face-3      markdown-header-face-6
```

Each of these inherits from the common `markdown-header-face`. So, to change all faces (e.g., a common font family or color) you can customize `markdown-header-face` directly. To change the face used for a specific heading level, customize that face individually.

 `markdown-header-face` inherits from `variable-pitch` by default, for contrast with the `default` face, which is a fixed width font by default. If you don't like the appearance of headings on your system, first ensure that you are setting the family of `variable-pitch` to something that pairs well with your `default` font.

3.2 Paragraphs

A paragraph in Markdown is one or more consecutive lines of text separated by one or more blank lines. Normal paragraphs should not be indented with spaces or tabs:

```
This is a paragraph.  It has two sentences.

This is another paragraph.  It also has two sentences.
```

3.3 Blockquotes

To produce a blockquote (<blockquote> in HTML), prefix each line with a right angle bracket (>), just as when quoting an email:

```
> This text will be enclosed in an HTML `<blockquote>` element.
```

Blockquotes may be nested, like so:

```
> Blockquote
>
> > Nested blockquote
```

To insert markup for a blockquote in Markdown Mode, use C-c C-s q (markdown-insert-blockquote). When transient-mark-mode is enabled, this command adds blockquote markup to the region, when active. Otherwise, it simply inserts markup for an empty blockquote and positions the point appropriately. The appropriate amount of indentation, if any, is calculated automatically given the surrounding context, but may be adjusted later using the region indentation commands described in the Indentation section below.

If you want to specifically operate on the region, whether or not transient-mark-mode and the region is active, you can use the region-specific command C-c C-s Q (markdown-blockquote-region).

Notice that the keybinding for this command, C-c C-s Q, is similar to C-c C-s q but the Q is uppercase. This pattern is also used with other paired or otherwise related commands in Markdown Mode, such as atx and setext heading insertion.

The region-specific functions such as markdown-blockquote-region are useful in some less obvious cases. For example, yanking text from the kill ring sets the mark at the beginning of the yanked text and leaves the point at the end. Therefore, even though the region is not active (i.e., it is not highlighted) the region does contain the yanked text and so C-c C-s Q will format it as a blockquote.

3.4 Lists

To produce an unordered list (`<ul>` in HTML), prefix each line with a list marker. Valid list marker characters are asterisks (*), hyphens (-), and plus signs (+):

```
* An item in a bulleted (unordered) list
* Another item in a bulleted list
```

Ordered lists (`<ol>` in HTML) are created by prefixing each line with a number followed by a period:

```
1. An item in an enumerated (ordered) list
2. Another item in an enumerated list
```

To create a *nested list*, use four spaces to indent the markers of subordinate items. You may change list markers if you wish to add more visual distinction. Note that it is the marker indentation that matters, not the whitespace following the marker.

```
*    An item in a bulleted (unordered) list

    *    A sub-item in a nested list

1234567890
```

 The four-space convention will show up again, for creating code blocks. For the broadest Markdown processor compatibility, it is recommended to always use four spaces for indenting and nesting elements.

> John Gruber conducted a Twitter Poll in July 2017 to ask which list markers were most popular among Markdown users. Out of 4,545 responses, the results were:
>
> - Asterisk (*): 42%
> - Hyphen (-): 54%
> - Plus (+): 4%
>
> Gruber noted that he uses all three at times, and that different characters can be used for different levels of nesting.

Creating and Editing Lists

New list items can be inserted with `M-RET` or `C-c C-j` (`markdown-insert-list-item`). This command determines the appropriate marker (one of the possible unordered list markers or the next number in sequence for an ordered list) and indentation level by examining nearby list items. If there is no list before or after the point, it starts a new list.

As with heading insertion, you may prefix `markdown-insert-list-item` by `C-u` to decrease the indentation by one level. Prefix this command by `C-u C-u` to increase the indentation by one level.

Existing list items (and their nested sub-items) can be moved up and down with `C-c <up>` and `C-c <down>` (`markdown-move-up` and `markdown-move-down`). List items can also be indented and outdented with `C-c <right>` and `C-c <left>` (`markdown-demote` and `markdown-promote`).

List Navigation

The same keys used for heading outline navigation (`C-c C-n`, `C-c C-p`, `C-c C-f`, `C-c C-b`, and `C-c C-u`) also work inside nested lists. See the Outline Navigation section for details.

List Customization

You can customize the default unordered list item marker and spacing by setting the variable `markdown-unordered-list-item-prefix`. Also, although it is not recommended to do so, if needed you can change the default indentation amount by setting `markdown-list-indent-width`.

`markdown-unordered-list-item-prefix`
String, default: " * ".

String to be inserted to create an unordered list item.

Example:

`(setq markdown-unordered-list-item-prefix "*   ")`

`markdown-list-indent-width`
Integer, default: 4.

Depth of indentation for lists when inserting, promoting, and demoting list items.

3.5 Paragraph & Block Movement

For the purposes of defining movement and marking commands, "paragraphs" in Markdown Mode include not only regular paragraphs as described above, but also paragraphs inside blockquotes, individual list items, headings, etc.

To move the point from one paragraph to another, use `M-{` and `M-}` (`markdown-backward-paragraph` and `markdown-forward-paragraph`). By default, these keys are bound to `forward-paragraph` and `backward-paragraph`, but the built-in Emacs functions are based on simple regular expressions that fail in Markdown files. To mark a paragraph, you can use `M-h` (`markdown-mark-paragraph`).

Markdown Mode also defines "block" movement commands, which are larger in scope and may contain multiple "paragraphs" in some cases. Blocks are considered to be entire lists, entire code blocks, and entire blockquotes. To move backward or forward by one block use `C-M-{` and `C-M-}` (`markdown-beginning-block` and `markdown-end-of-block`). To mark a block, use `C-c M-h` (`markdown-mark-block`). To narrow the buffer to the current block, use `C-x n b` (`markdown-narrow-to-block`) and to widen again use `C-x n w` (`widen`).

To compare paragraph and block movement, consider some specific examples. In terms of list items, paragraph movement moves item-by-item, regardless of the list item level. On the other hand, block movement moves across the entire list. Suppose the point is at the block, as in the following example:

```
Paragraph

- item 1
- item 2
- item 3
▊
```

Moving backwards by "paragraph" with `M-{` first moves the point back to the marker for item 3, then back to the marker for item 2, and so on. Moving backwards by one "block" with `C-M-{`, on the other hand, moves the point immediately to the marker for item 1.

Next, consider a blockquote with multiple paragraphs as in the following example:

```
Regular paragraph

> blockquote paragraph 1
>
> blockquote paragraph 2.
▊
```

Moving backward by one paragraph leaves the point at the > before blockquote paragraph 2 while moving backward by one block moves over the entire blockquote and leaves the point at the > before blockquote paragraph 1.

3.6 Indentation

The Tab Key

Markdown Mode attempts to be flexible in how it handles indentation. When you press `TAB` (`markdown-cycle`) repeatedly, the point will cycle through several possible indentation levels corresponding to locations you might have in mind. For example, you may want to start a new list item, continue a list item with hanging indentation, indent for a nested `<pre>` block, and so on.

```
- list item
    - nested list item
█
5   1 2 3   4
```

The numbers in the block above represent the indentation positions that are cycled through following a nested list when the point is at the block above position 5. In order, these positions would be appropriate for 1) starting a new nested list item, 2) continuing the nested list item with indentation past the marker, 3) starting a list item with a deeper level of nesting, 4) adding a nested indented code block, and 5) starting a new list item at the top level of the list.

If you so desire, you can fully customize this behavior by writing your own indentation function and setting the variable `markdown-indent-function` appropriately.

`markdown-indent-function`
    Function, default: `markdown-indent-line`.

    Function to use for automatic indentation.

The Backspace Key

When DEL or <backspace> (`markdown-outdent-or-delete`) is pressed at the beginning of the non-whitespace portion of a line, text will be outdented similarly, but in the opposite direction as indentation.

The Return Key

When the point is at the end of a (potentially nested) list item, code block, etc. and you press RET (`markdown-enter-key`), what happens next depends on the value of `markdown-indent-on-enter`. As an example, consider the following nested list.

```
- list item
    - nested list item█
```

When `markdown-indent-on-enter` is `nil`, the point will move to column 0 of the following line:

```
- list item
    - nested list item
▮
```

When `markdown-indent-on-enter` is set to `t`, the point will be positioned for continuing your nested list.

```
- list item
    - nested list item
    ▮
```

In this scenario, if you wanted to continue your existing (now line-wrapped) list item with hanging indentation, simply press TAB to indent to the next logical position.

```
- list item
    - nested list item
      ▮
```

Finally, when `markdown-indent-on-enter` is set to `indent-and-new-item`, Markdown Mode will automatically insert a new list item. With this setting, pressing RET again removes the empty list item and leaves a blank line. If you want to insert a single literal newline, you can use `quoted-insert` via C-q C-j.

```
- list item
    - nested list item
    - ▮
```

markdown-indent-on-enter
: nil, t, or indent-and-new-item, default: t.

    When non-nil, automatically indent new lines when the enter key is pressed. When set to indent-and-new-item, additionally insert a new list item marker if the point was in a list item.

Shifting the Region

Text in the region can be outdented or indented as a single block using C-c < and C-c > (markdown-outdent-region and markdown-indent-region). Text in the region will be shifted to the next indentation point calculated in the current context, as discussed above.

> The region indent and outdent keybindings are the same as those for the corresponding commands in python-mode.

3.7 Code Blocks

Code blocks in Markdown are formatted by prefixing each line with four spaces:

```
#include <stdio.h>
int main()
{
    printf("hello, world\n");
    return 0;
}
```

1234567890

To begin a new code block press C-c C-s p (markdown-insert-pre), where p refers to the HTML <pre> tag used to format such a block. When transient-mark-mode is enabled, this command also works on the region, when active, or begins a new code block otherwise.

If you want to specifically operate on the region, whether it is highlighted with transient-mark-mode or not, you can use the region-specific command C-c C-s P (markdown-pre-region). So, as with other commands, the lowercase and uppercase keybindings are related.

> Region-specific commands such as this one are useful when you have just yanked some text and want to format it, say, as a code block. Upon yanking, the mark moved to the beginning of the yanked text and so the region is already set appropriately.

> In addition to indented code blocks, or pre blocks, Markdown Mode also supports several variations referred to as fenced code blocks. Rather than being indented, fenced code blocks are surrounded above and below by strings of tildes or backquotes. We will return to fenced code blocks later, in the Extensions chapter.

3.8 Horizontal Rules

Horizontal rules, corresponding to <hr> tags in HTML, are created in Markdown by placing three or more hyphens, asterisks, or underscores on a line by themselves. You may use spaces between the characters if you prefer, but the characters cannot be mixed. Each of the following lines will produce a horizontal rule:

```
---
- - -
* * *
_____
```

To insert a horizontal rule, press C-c C-s - (markdown-insert-hr). Markdown Mode allows you to define several horizontal rules of decreasing prominence in a list variable named markdown-hr-strings. By default, this command inserts the first string in markdown-hr-strings—the most prominent one. With a C-u prefix, insert the last string. With a numeric prefix N, insert the string in position N (starting at 1). The list of strings inserted by Markdown Mode can be customized by redefining the variable markdown-hr-strings.

markdown-hr-strings
> List of strings.
>
> Strings to use when inserting horizontal rules.

> Different strings will not be distinguished when converted to HTML—they will all be converted to <hr> tags—but they may add visual distinction and style to plain text documents. To maintain notions of promotion and demotion, these should be ordered from largest to smallest.

> To insert a specific horizontal rule from the markdown-hr-strings list, use a prefix argument to C-c C-s -, as in C-# C-c C-s - where # is the index of the string in the list.

> In the default `markdown-hr-strings` list, the longest two strings are 79 characters long, rather than 80 characters long, to prevent a line wrap indicator from appearing in the right fringe when the window is exactly 80 characters wide. However, the list is fully customizable and if you prefer an 80-character-wide string you can set this variable in your local configuration.

3.9 Emphasis: Italic & Bold

To emphasize text in Markdown, surround it with asterisks or underscores. For *italics*, use single asterisks or underscores:

`*italic*` or `_italic_`

Similarly, enclose **bold** text between two asterisks or two underscores:

`**bold**` or `__bold__`

In Markdown Mode, `C-c C-s i` (`markdown-insert-italic`) inserts markup to make the region or a word italic. If `transient-mark-mode` is on and there is an active region, it wraps the region in italic markup. Else, if the point is at a non-italic word, make the word italic, or if the point is at an italic word or phrase, remove (toggle) the markup. Otherwise, simply insert italic markup and place the point in the middle.

Similarly, use `C-c C-s b` (`markdown-insert-bold`) for bold text. This command works in exactly the same way as `markdown-insert-italic`.

Like the three possible list markers, the use of asterisks or underscores for italic or bold text is a personal preference in Markdown. Markdown Mode lets you customize the default choice for inserting new markup via two variables described below.

> Brett Terpstra, in his Write better Markdown style guide, recommends maintaining a consistent style with respect to asterisks and underscores throughout a document. For example, you might always use underscores for italics and asterisks for bold.

> You can also *toggle* between asterisks and underscores using the promotion and demotion commands, `C-c C--` and `C-c C-=` (`markdown-promote` and `markdown-demote`).

> Markdown processors differ as to how they handle inter-word underscores. When Markdown.pl encounters `_dis_functional`, it assumes you intend to italicize "dis". However, if you are writing technical documentation, perhaps you have a variable named `state_space_dimension`. Unless you format that as inline code, then the middle word—`space`—would become italicized. GitHub Flavored Markdown re-defines this behavior so that inter-word underscores do not trigger italics. Markdown Mode includes a special mode, GitHub Flavored Markdown Mode or `gfm-mode`, and among other differences, it uses the GitHub convention for underscores. This mode is described in the section on GitHub Flavored Markdown in the Extensions chapter.

`markdown-italic-underscore`
: Boolean, default: `nil`.

    Set to a non-`nil` value to use underscores instead of asterisks when inserting markup for italic text.

    Example:

    ```
    (setq markdown-italic-underscore t)
    ```

`markdown-bold-underscore`
: Boolean, default: `nil`.

    Set to a non-`nil` value to use two underscores instead of two asterisks when inserting markup for bold text.

    Example:

    ```
    (setq markdown-bold-underscore nil)
    ```

3.10 Inline Code

To mark up inline source code, for command names, file names, etc., place the text between backquotes (`` ` ``) like so:

```
This is inline code: `printf("hello, world\n");`
```

To insert inline code in Markdown Mode, use `C-c C-s c` (`markdown-insert-code`). This command works for both insertion and toggling and it uses the region when appropriate, just like the bold and italic commands.

> Because Markdown is often used for technical documentation (e.g., README files on GitHub), Markdown Mode also provides `C-c C-s k` (`markdown-insert-kbd`) for inserting HTML `<kbd>` tags, for which there is no Markdown equivalent. In terms of font lock, `<kbd>` tags are treated like inline code but of course they may be styled differently on websites and elsewhere.

3.11 Links & Images

To create simple links, you can simply place a URL or email address inside angle brackets:

```
<https://www.gnu.org/software/emacs/>
<bug-gnu-emacs@gnu.org>
```

To create hyperlinks—text with an associated URL—place the link text in square brackets followed by the URL in parentheses:

```
[Link text](http://link.url/)
```

Optionally, you can add "title text" (for the HTML `title` attribute) to the link which will appear when the user's mouse pointer hovers over the link:

```
[Link text](http://link.url/ "Title text")
```

A similar syntax is used for images: just add an exclamation point (!) before the square bracket. There is no equivalent of link text for images, so instead the text in square brackets will be used as the "alt text" (for the HTML `alt` attribute):

```
![Alt text](http://link.url/image.jpg "Title text")
```

In Markdown Mode, links of the above form are referred to as "inline links" because the URL is written out in full inline in the Markdown text. On the other hand, "reference links" allow you to keep the text clean and define the URLs later:

```
You can define short reference link like this:
[link text here][1]

[1]: http://link.url/

You can still include a title, like this:
[link text here][ref]

[ref]: http://link.url/ "Title text"

Finally, you can use implicitly defined reference links
where the reference label is the same as the link text:
[link text][]

[link text]: http://link.url/
```

Inserting Links & Images

For links, `C-c C-l` (markdown-insert-link) is the general command for inserting new link markup or editing existing link markup interactively. This command can be used to insert links of any form: either inline links, reference links, or plain URLs in angle brackets. The URL or reference label, link text, and optional title are provided through a series of prompts. The type of link is determined by which values are provided:

- Given a URL and link text, insert an inline link: `[text](url)`.
- Given a `[reference]` and link text, insert a reference link: `[text][reference]`.
- Given only link text, insert an implicit reference link: `[text][]`.
- Given only a URL, insert a plain URL: `<url>`.

Similarly, `C-c C-i` (markdown-insert-image) is a general command for inserting or editing image markup interactively. As with the link insertion command, through a series of interactive prompts you can insert either an inline or reference image:

- Given a URL and alt text, insert an inline image: `![alt](url)`.
- Given a `[reference]` and alt text, insert a reference image: `![alt][reference]`.

If there is an existing link or image at the point, these commands will edit the existing markup rather than inserting new markup. Otherwise, if `transient-mark-mode` is on and there is an active region, these commands use the region as either the default URL (if it seems to be a URL) or link text value otherwise. In that case, the region will be replaced by the link.

If a reference label is given that is not yet defined, you will be prompted for the URL and optional title and the reference definition will be inserted according to the value of `markdown-reference-location`. If a title is given, it will be added to the end of the reference definition and will be used to populate the HTML `title` attribute when exported.

You can use `C-c C-d` (`markdown-do`) to jump between reference labels and reference definitions. If more than one link uses the same reference label, a window will be shown with clickable buttons for jumping to each link. Pressing `TAB` or `S-TAB` cycles between buttons in this window.

> Note that interactive functions `C-c C-l` and `C-c C-i` can be used to convert links and images from one type to another (inline, reference, or plain URL) by selectively adding or removing properties via the interactive prompts.

> As an example, suppose you have an inline link of the form `[text](url)` and want to convert it to a plain URL link as in `<url>`. If you press `C-c C-l` and leave the URL as is when prompted but remove the link text, then a plain URL, as in `<url>`, will be inserted in place of the inline link. If you removed the URL instead, then you would be prompted for a reference label.

Following Links

Links in Markdown Mode are clickable and clicking one will open the URL in the default browser. To follow a link using the keyboard, press `C-c C-o` (`markdown-follow-thing-at-point`) when the point is on an inline or reference link. Use `M-p` and `M-n` (`markdown-previous-link` and `markdown-next-link`) to quickly jump to the previous or next link of any type.

URL Hiding

Markdown Mode makes it possible to hide URLs for inline and reference links, which can make your text more readable. This feature can be toggled as needed using `C-c C-x C-l` (`markdown-toggle-url-hiding`) or from the Markdown menu. When URL hiding is enabled, the URL components of links will be displayed as a single, customizable character (∞ by default). That is, URLs will appear as [link](∞) instead of [link](long/url).

URL hiding is accomplished in Emacs using *composition*, so the URLs are still part of the buffer. To change the placeholder (composition) character used, set the variable markdown-url-compose-char.

When URL hiding is enabled, the link properties will be displayed in the minibuffer along with a hint to use C-c C-l for editing the link. You can also edit a URL directly by deleting the final parenthesis, which disables fontification of the link and thus removes the composition property. Finally, you can also hover your mouse pointer over the link text to see the URL.

markdown-hide-urls
:   Boolean, default: nil.

    Determines whether URL and reference labels are hidden for inline and reference links. This can be toggled interactively using C-c C-x C-l (markdown-toggle-url-hiding).

markdown-url-compose-char
:   Character, default: ∞.

    Placeholder character for hidden URLs. Depending on your font, some other good choices are ... and #.

> The interactive link and image commands C-c C-l and C-c C-i are especially useful when markup or URL hiding is enabled, in which case it is more difficult to edit URLs.

Link & Image Customizations

Certain aspects of link and image insertion can be customized, such as the default location of reference links and the protocol schemes of URLs that should be recognized automatically.

markdown-reference-location
:   immediately, header, subtree, or end, default: header.

    Determines where to insert reference definitions. The possible locations are the end of the document (end), after the current block (immediately), the end of the current subtree (subtree), or before the next heading (header).

    Example:

```
(setq markdown-reference-location 'end)
```

markdown-uri-types
    List of strings.

    A list of protocol schemes ("http", "ftp", etc.) for URLs that Markdown Mode should highlight.

Inline Image Display

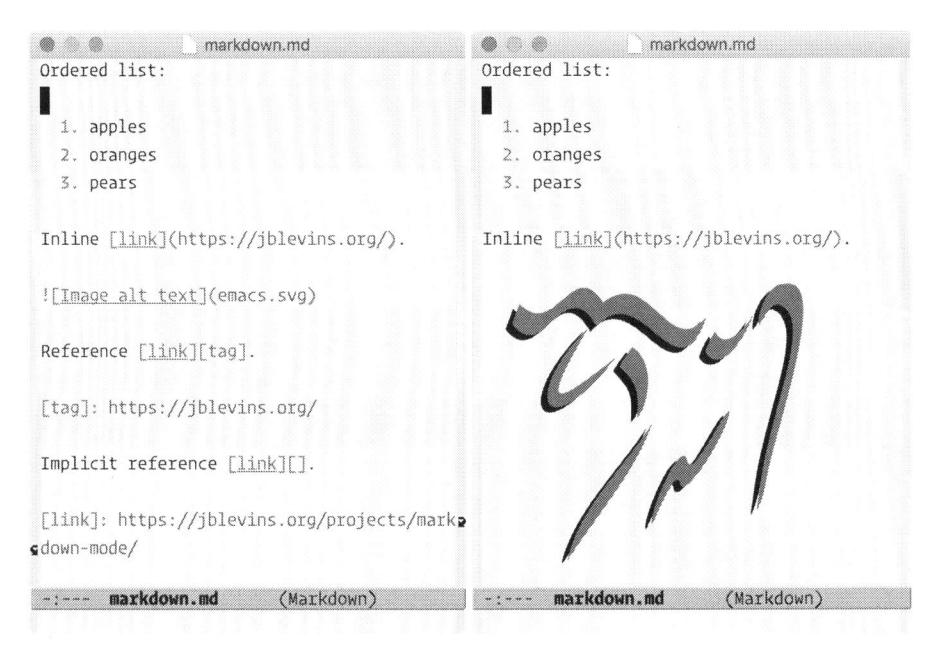

Inline Image Display in Markdown Mode

Local images associated with image links may be displayed inline in the buffer by pressing `C-c C-x C-i` or `M-x markdown-toggle-inline-images`. This is a toggle command, so pressing this again will remove inline images.

3.12 Line Breaks

In Markdown, whitespace at the end of a line is meaningful. Adding two trailing spaces at the end of a line creates a hard line break. Markdown Mode highlights these spaces to draw attention to possibly spurious whitespace. Markdown Mode also respects hard line breaks when filling paragraphs.

3.13 Killing Elements

Press `C-c C-k` (`markdown-kill-thing-at-point`) to kill the thing at point and add the most important text, without markup, to the kill ring. Possible entities to kill include (roughly in order of precedence): inline code, headings, horizontal rules, links (adds the link text to kill ring), images (adds the alt text to kill ring), plain URLs, email addresses, bold, italics, reference definitions (adds URL to kill ring), footnote markers and text (kills both the marker and text, adds text to kill ring), and list items. See the following table for a summary.

Killed Entity	Kill Ring
`` `code` ``	"code"
`# Heading`	"Heading"
`-----`	nil
`[text](url)`	"text"
`[text][ref]`	"text"
`![alt](url)`	"alt"
`![alt][ref]`	"alt"
`<url>`	"url"
`_text_`	"text"
`**text**`	"text"
`[ref]: url`	"url"
`[^fn], [^fn]: footnote`	"footnote"
`* List item`	"List item"

3.14 Markdown Do

Markdown Mode defines `C-c C-d` (`markdown-do`), a command for doing something sensible with the object at the point. Depending on the context, it does the following:

- Jumps between reference links and reference definitions.
- Jumps between footnote markers and footnote text.
- Toggles the completion status of GFM task list items (checkboxes).

> The Markdown Do command has evolved over the past three versions of Markdown Mode. It derives from a previous command named `markdown-jump`, which was previously bound to `C-c C-j` in Markdown Mode 2.1. It was later moved to `C-c C-l` in Markdown Mode 2.2 to allow using `C-c C-j` (in addition to `M-RET`) for inserting list items, as in AUCTeX mode. In Markdown Mode 2.3, this command has been imbued with additional functionality, rebranded as `markdown-do`, and moved to `C-c C-d` to make way for the new interactive link editing command `C-c C-l`.

3.15 Markup Promotion & Demotion

Markdown Mode allows certain markup (headings, for example) to be *promoted* and *demoted*. Press `C-c C--` or `C-c <left>` (`markdown-promote`) to promote the element at the point if possible. Similarly, `C-c C-=` or `C-c <right>` (`markdown-demote`) to demote the element at the point.

Headings, horizontal rules, and list items can be promoted and demoted, as well as bold and italic text. For headings, promotion means *decreasing* the level (i.e., from `<h2>` to `<h1>`) while demotion means *increasing* the level (i.e., from `<h2>` to `<h3>`). For horizontal rules, promotion and demotion mean moving backward or forward through the `markdown-hr-strings` list. For bold and italic text, promotion and demotion mean switching the markup from underscores to asterisks and back.

> To promote or demote markup at the point, where applicable, use `C-c C--` and `C-c C-=`. To remember the promotion and demotion commands, note that `-` is for decreasing the level, and `=` (on the same key as `+`) is for increasing the level. Similarly, the left and right arrow keys indicate the direction in which the atx heading markup will move when promoting or demoting.

> You can change the level of a heading level two ways:
>
> 1. Using markup cycling, with either `C-c C--` and `C-c C-=` or the alternatives `C-c <left>` and `C-c <right>`.
> 2. By re-issuing a heading insertion command when the point is at a heading. For example, `C-c C-s 4` will replace the current heading (of any level) with a level-four heading.

3.16 Markup Completion

Complete markup refers to markup in normalized form. This means, for example, that the underlined portion of a setext heading is the same length as the heading text, or that the number of leading and trailing hash marks of an atx heading are equal and that there is no extra whitespace. To complete any incomplete markup at the point, press C-c C-] (markdown-complete).

Suppose a buffer contains the following headings, one with an underline that is too short and another with extra whitespace and a missing hash mark:

```
Heading 1
===

##   Heading 2 #
```

Markup completion via C-c C-] will adjust them as follows:

```
Heading 1
=========

## Heading 2 ##
```

3.17 Markdown Maintenance Commands

Markdown Mode also provides some *global* maintenance commands under the C-c C-c prefix for checking references, cleaning up list numbers, and completing markup in the buffer.

C-c C-c c (markdown-check-refs)
   Checks the buffer for undefined references. If there are any, a small buffer will open with a list of undefined references and the line numbers on which they appear. Selecting a reference from this list and pressing RET will insert an empty reference definition at the end of the buffer. Selecting the line number instead will move the point to the location of the undefined reference.

C-c C-c n (markdown-cleanup-list-numbers)
> Renumbers any ordered lists in the buffer that are out of sequence. Note that the sequence is not important for rendering HTML—a list with numbers `1.`, `1.`, ..., `1.` is perfectly fine—but this command is useful if you prefer to also maintain accurate plain text numbering.

C-c C-c] (markdown-complete-buffer)
> Completes all heading markup and normalizes all horizontal rules in the buffer.

* * *

4. Extensions

4.1 Fenced Code Blocks

In addition to indented code blocks, Markdown Mode also supports *fenced code blocks*. Although fenced code blocks are not universally supported by all Markdown processors, a primary advantage is that they allow authors to indicate the name of the language of the source code contained within, to assist with syntax highlighting and CSS styling. They also remove the need to maintain the four-space leading indentation, which can make editing code blocks more difficult.

GFM Code Blocks

The first type of fenced code blocks supported by Markdown Mode are those used by GitHub-Flavored Markdown (GFM). These blocks begin and end with three consecutive backquotes on separate lines. After the opening three backquotes, you may give an optional language identifier, optionally separated by whitespace. These are referred to in Markdown Mode simply as GFM code blocks:

```
```
a one-line code block
```
```

```
```python
print("hello, world")
```
```

```
``` Ruby
puts("hello, world")
```
```

To insert a GFM code block interactively in Markdown Mode, press `C-c C-s C` (`markdown-insert-gfm-code-block`). You will be presented with a minibuffer prompt asking for an optional programming language name. Markdown Mode includes a large list of known languages to select from. The default value will be the most recently used language.

The GFM programming language prompt uses `completing-read`, which has several useful keybindings such as M-n and M-p to select the next or previous elements and M-s and M-r to select the next or previous elements matching a partially complete string.

> Since it uses `completing-read`, programming language selection will also work with `ido`, `ivy`, and `helm`.

Another way to insert a GFM code block is to use the *electric backquote* feature, which is enabled by default. When this setting is enabled, pressing the backquote key (`` ` ``) three times triggers `markdown-insert-gfm-code-block` automatically. At present, this feature is only enabled in `gfm-mode`.

markdown-gfm-use-electric-backquote
Boolean, default: `t`.

When non-`nil`, trigger interactive insertion of GFM code blocks when the backquote key is pressed three times.

Additionally, you can augment the list of known language names by setting `markdown-gfm-additional-languages` and you can indicate a preference for lowercase language identifiers with `markdown-gfm-downcase-languages`.

markdown-gfm-additional-languages
List of strings, default: `nil`.

This variable contains additional languages to make available, aside from those predefined in `markdown-gfm-recognized-languages`, when inserting GFM code blocks. Language strings must be trimmed of whitespace and not contain curly braces. They may be of arbitrary capitalization.

Example:

```
(setq markdown-gfm-additional-languages '("Texinfo" "Zimbu"))
```

markdown-gfm-downcase-languages
Boolean, default: `t`.

When non-`nil`, apply `downcase` to suggested programming language names to convert them to lowercase.

`markdown-spaces-after-code-fence`

Integer, default: 1.

Number of space characters to insert between an opening code fence and the optional programming language name.

Example:

```
(setq markdown-spaces-after-code-fence 0)
```

Tilde-Fenced Code Blocks

The second type of fenced code blocks supported by Markdown Mode are tilde-fenced code blocks. Markdown processors supporting this extension include PHP Markdown Extra, Pandoc, and Leanpub among others. The block opens with *at least three* tildes (~) and closes with at least as many tildes as it was opened with (but possibly more):

```
~~~~~~~~~~~~~~~~~~~~~
a one-line code block
~~~~~~~~~~~~~~~~~~~~~
```

> Markdown Mode supports font-lock and indirect editing of tilde-fenced code blocks, but it does not yet include a dedicated command for inserting them.

Language Strings

Some processors allow you to specify the language of the source code using attribute lists of various formats, as in the following examples. Markdown Mode takes an inclusive approach to highlighting such blocks by allowing optional braces, periods, `lang` attributes, and so on:

```
```{r, eval=FALSE}
summary(gdp)
```


~~~~~~~~~~~~~~~~~~ .html
<p>hello, world</p>
~~~~~~~~~~~~~~~~~~


~~~~{.python}
print("hello, world")
~~~~


~~~~~~~ {: lang=fortran }
program main
  print *, 'hello, world'
end program main
~~~~~~~~~~~~~~~~~~~~~~~~~
```

Native Font Lock and Indirect Editing

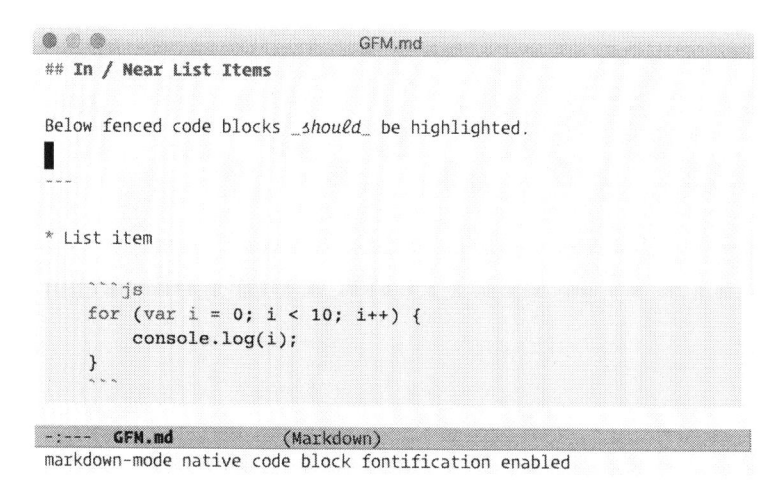

Native Font Lock for a JavaScript Code Block

Markdown Mode can also optionally perform native syntax highlighting of source code in fenced code blocks. This works for GFM and tilde-fenced code blocks for which a language name has been specified. You can toggle this mode with either C-c C-x C-f or

M-x markdown-toggle-fontify-code-blocks-natively and you can set the default behavior by customizing the variable markdown-fontify-code-blocks-natively.

markdown-fontify-code-blocks-natively
    Boolean, default: nil.

    When non-nil, fontify code in code blocks using the native major mode. This only works for fenced code blocks where the language is specified and where Markdown Mode can automatically determine the appropriate mode to use.

Additionally, if you have the edit-indirect package installed Markdown Mode can open code blocks for editing in an "indirect" buffer with the native major mode enabled. To do this, press C-c ' (markdown-edit-code-block). A new window will open with the contents of the code block and with the guessed major mode enabled. The code block in the Markdown buffer will be highlighted to indicate that it is being edited elsewhere. When you are finished editing in the indirect buffer, press C-c C-c (edit-indirect-commit) to "commit" any changes and update the Markdown buffer or press C-c C-k (edit-indirect-abort) to cancel and ignore any changes.

Editing a GFM Code Block in an Indirect Buffer

Both native font lock and indirect editing require Markdown Mode to try to determine the appropriate mode to use for each language identifier. Sometimes this is straightforward. For example, shell maps to shell-mode and emacs-lisp maps to emacs-lisp-mode. In other cases, the language and mode names may not agree or a different mode may be desired. The language-to-mode mapping may be customized as needed by setting the variable `markdown-code-lang-modes`.

`markdown-code-lang-modes`
>Association list.
>
>An alist mapping languages to their major modes. Keys are strings representing language names and values are major mode symbols. For example, a default element of this alist is (`"sqlite"` . `sql-mode`), which instructs Markdown Mode to use `sql-mode` to highlight and edit `sqlite` code blocks.

In practice, the language-to-mode mapping is handled by the `markdown-get-lang-mode` function, which looks for a defined function satisfying one of the following forms, in order, where `<lang>` represents the language keyword specified for the code block:

1. An entry with key `<lang>` specified in `markdown-code-lang-modes`.
2. A function named `<lang>-mode`.

> As an example, suppose you have a code block with language name `matlab`. By default, there is no element of `markdown-code-lang-modes` with key `matlab`, so Markdown Mode checks to see if `matlab-mode` is defined. If so, it will be used for syntax highlighting of the code block and also for indirect editing of the code block.

4.2 Footnotes

Footnotes are another common and reasonably standardized extension to Markdown. Footnotes consist of an inline marker, such as `[^fn]` and a definition, where the footnote text is given:

```
Paragraph text.[^fn]

[^fn]: Footnote text.
```

To insert a footnote in Markdown Mode press C-c C-s f (markdown-insert-footnote). This inserts a footnote marker such as [^1] at the point, inserts a footnote definition below, and positions the point for typing the footnote text. Footnotes inserted this way are numbered, and the counter advances automatically.

> This footnote syntax is an extension to Markdown and although it is in common use, it is not supported by all processors.

As with reference links, you can customize the location of footnote definitions. Similarly, you can use C-c C-d (markdown-do) to jump between footnote markers and footnote definitions.

markdown-footnote-location
    immediately, header, subtree, or end, default: end.

    Determines where to insert footnote text. The set of location options is the same as for markdown-reference-location: the possible locations are the end of the document (end), after the current block (immediately), the end of the current subtree (subtree), or before the next heading (header).

    Example:

    ```
    (setq markdown-footnote-location 'subtree)
    ```

> Markdown Mode also includes basic font lock support for Pandoc's *inline footnotes*:
>
>   Here is an inline footnote.^[Footnote text here.]
>
> This is, however, a processor-specific extension.

4.3 Definition Lists

Several Markdown processors, such as PHP Markdown Extra, Pandoc, MultiMarkdown, and Python Markdown, support an extension called *definition lists*, which correspond to <dl> tags in HTML. A simple definition list begins with a term followed by a newline and a colon at the beginning of the next line, which separates the definition:

```
Term
:   Definition
```

In HTML, this becomes:

```
<dl>
<dt>Term</dt>
<dd><p>Definition</p></dd>
</dl>
```

As with many words in a typical dictionary, you can specify multiple definitions per term. To borrow an example from the PHP Markdown Extra documentation:

```
Apple
:   Pomaceous fruit of plants of the genus Malus in
    the family Rosaceae.
:   An American computer company.

Orange
:   The fruit of an evergreen tree of the genus Citrus.
```

Markdown Mode provides basic syntax highlighting and filling for definition lists, and some of the list-related commands previously described also work for definition lists. For example, you can move items up and down with `C-c <up>` (`markdown-move-up`) and `C-c <down>` (`markdown-move-down`). However, Markdown Mode does not yet provide dedicated commands for inserting or otherwise manipulating definition lists.

4.4 Comments

Although there is no official syntax for comments in Markdown, since it is most often converted to HTML the most natural comment syntax is that used in HTML: `<!-- comment -->`. You can use the usual Emacs commands in Markdown Mode for commenting and uncommenting:

M-; (`comment-dwim`)
: Insert or align comment on the current line. If `transient-mark-mode` is on and the region is active, invoke `comment-region` instead (unless the region is a block of comments, in which case invoke `uncomment-region`).

`C-x C-;` **`(comment-line)`**
: Comment or uncomment the current line.

`C-u M-;` **`(comment-kill)`**
: Kill a comment on the current line.

4.5 Task List Items (Checkboxes)

GitHub Flavored Markdown (GFM) defines a syntax for task lists (i.e., checkboxes) which is a straightforward and backward-compatible modification of Markdown's unordered list syntax.

```
- [ ] Incomplete task
- [x] Completed task
```

By default, Markdown Mode activates these checkboxes so that they can be clicked using the mouse, or by pressing `RET` when the point is at a checkbox. You can also toggle checkboxes using either the dedicated toggle command `C-c C-x C-x` (markdown-toggle-gfm-checkbox) or the context-specific command `C-c C-d` (markdown-do).

`markdown-make-gfm-checkboxes-buttons`
: Boolean, default: `t`.

    Determines whether GitHub Flavored Markdown style task lists (checkboxes) should be turned into buttons that can be toggled with `mouse-1` or `RET`. When non-`nil`, buttons are enabled. This works both in `markdown-mode` and `gfm-mode`.

`markdown-gfm-uppercase-checkbox`
: Boolean, default: `nil`.

    When non-`nil`, complete GFM task list items with the uppercase [X] instead of the lowercase [x]. This is primarily useful for compatibility with Org Mode, which doesn't recognize the lowercase form. GFM, however, supports both forms.

4.6 Subscripts and Superscripts

Pandoc and MultiMarkdown, among other Markdown processors, support extensions for subscripts and superscripts. Markdown Mode supports this syntax as well. Superscripts may be written by placing carets (^) immediately before and after the text. Similarly, subscripts may be written by placing tildes (~) immediately before and after the text.

```
H~2~O is a liquid.   2^10^ is 1024.
```

4.7 Metadata

Markdown Mode provides font lock support for several common metadata formats, such as those supported by MultiMarkdown, Pandoc, and GitHub.

One of the simplest forms is email-style metadata that must appear at the beginning of the file. This metadata format is supported by MultiMarkdown and some blog generation systems.

```
title: Guide to Markdown Mode for Emacs
author: Jason R. Blevins
```

Markdown Mode also supports Pandoc metadata, which also must appear at the beginning of a file and is indicated by percent signs:

```
% title
% author(s) (separated by semicolons)
% date
```

Finally, Markdown Mode supports YAML and TOML metadata blocks. YAML and TOML metadata blocks begin with a line of three hyphens (---) and end with either a line of three hyphens (---) or three dots (...). Pandoc, GitHub, and Jekyll all support YAML metadata.

```
---
title: Guide to Markdown Mode for Emacs
author: Jason R. Blevins
tags: Emacs, markdown, markdown-mode, writing, plain text
---
```

Some website generators, such as Hugo, also support TOML metadata.

```
---
title = "Guide to Markdown Mode for Emacs"
author = "Jason R. Blevins"
---
```

Optionally, Markdown Mode allows YAML and TOML metadata to occur anywhere in the document. This is disabled by default, for performance reasons, but you can customize `markdown-use-pandoc-style-yaml-metadata` to enable it.

`markdown-use-pandoc-style-yaml-metadata`
    Boolean, default: `nil`.

    When non-`nil`, allow YAML and TOML metadata anywhere in the document.

4.8 Wiki Links

Markdown Mode also supports syntax highlighting for `[[Wiki Links]]`. Note that wiki links are an extension to Markdown and are not supported by all processors, so this support is disabled by default. Support can be toggled with `M-x markdown-toggle-wiki-links` or by setting `markdown-enable-wiki-links`.

To insert a wiki link, use `C-c C-s w` (`markdown-insert-wiki-link`). If transient-mark-mode is on and there is an active region, this command will use the region as the link text. If the point is at a word, use the word as the link text. If there is no active region and the point is not at word, it will simply insert empty wiki link brackets.

Wiki links may be followed by pressing `C-c C-o` when the point is at a wiki link. This will find the corresponding file in the current window, by default, or in another window when the `C-u` prefix is given. As with regular links, you can use `M-p` and `M-n` to quickly jump to the previous and next links (including other kinds of links).

Aliased or piped wiki links of the form `[[link text|PageName]]` are also supported. Since some wiki engines reverse these components, set `markdown-wiki-link-alias-first` to nil to treat them as `[[PageName|link text]]` instead.

By default, Markdown Mode only searches for target files in the current directory. Sequential subdirectory search can be enabled by setting `markdown-wiki-link-search-subdirectories` to a non-nil value. Similarly, sequential parent directory search can be enabled by setting `markdown-wiki-link-search-parent-directories` to a non-nil value.

markdown-enable-wiki-links
> Boolean, default: `nil`.
>
> Enable or disable syntax highlighting for wiki links. Set this variable to a non-nil value to enable wiki link support. Wiki link support can also be toggled interactively using the function `markdown-toggle-wiki-links`.
>
> *Example:*
>
> `(setq markdown-enable-wiki-links t)`

markdown-wiki-link-alias-first
> Boolean, default: `t`.
>
> Set to a non-nil value to treat aliased wiki links like `[[link text|PageName]]`. When set to `nil`, they will be treated as `[[PageName|link text]]`.

markdown-link-space-sub-char
> String, default: `"_"` in `markdown-mode` and `"-"` in `gfm-mode`.
>
> Character to replace spaces when mapping wiki links to filenames. For example, use an underscore for compatibility with the Python Markdown WikiLinks extension. In GFM Mode, this is set to `"-"` to conform with the GitHub wiki link conventions.
>
> *Example:*
>
> `(setq markdown-link-space-sub-char "-")`

markdown-wiki-link-fontify-missing
> Boolean, default: `nil`.
>
> When non-nil, set wiki link faces according to the existence or absence of target files.
>
> *Example:*
>
> `(setq markdown-wiki-link-fontify-missing t)`

> ⚠ Note that this is expensive because it requires checking each linked file every time the buffer changes or the user switches windows. It is disabled by default because it may cause lag when typing on slower machines.

`markdown-wiki-link-search-subdirectories`
   Boolean, default: `nil`.

   When non-`nil`, search for wiki link targets in subdirectories. This is the default search behavior for GitHub, so this variable is automatically set to `t` in `gfm-mode`.

`markdown-wiki-link-search-parent-directories`
   Boolean, default: `nil`.

   When non-`nil`, search for wiki link targets in parent directories. This is the default search behavior of the Ikiwiki engine.

4.9 Mathematical Expressions (LaTeX)

LaTeX Math in Markdown Mode

Syntax highlighting for mathematical expressions written in LaTeX can be toggling with C-c C-x C-e (`markdown-toggle-math`), where the final e is for *equation*. Importantly, this is *not* full LaTeX support. It only involves font lock and only for expressions delimited by $..$, $$..$$, or \[..\] are supported; this does not yet include dedicated commands for inserting or otherwise manipulating mathematical markup.

```
A simple equation for a line in $\mathbb{R}^2$:

\[ y = mx + b \]

Again, but with dollar signs:

$$ y = mx + b $$
```

Alternatively, you can enable this by default by setting `markdown-enable-math` to a non-nil value. You can do this on a file-by-file basis using File Local Variables. Or you can enable this setting globally, via `M-x customize` or by placing `(setq markdown-enable-math t)` in your startup file. In that case, you should restart Emacs or call `markdown-reload-extensions`.

`markdown-enable-math`
    Boolean, default: `nil`.

    Enable syntax highlighting for LaTeX expressions.

4.10 GitHub Flavored Markdown (GFM) Mode

GitHub Flavored Markdown is a dialect of Markdown developed for use on GitHub. A GitHub Flavored Markdown Mode for Emacs is also available as `gfm-mode` and is part of the Markdown Mode package.

The GitHub implementation of Markdown differs slightly from standard Markdown in that it supports things like different behavior for underscores inside of words, automatic linking of URLs, strikethrough text, and fenced code blocks with an optional language keyword. Many of these extensions have been discussed already, but here we address them collectively in relation to `gfm-mode`.

On GitHub, the GFM-specific features above apply to `README.md` files, wiki pages, and other Markdown-formatted files in repositories on GitHub. GitHub also enables additional features for writing on the site (for issues, pull requests, messages, etc.) that are further extensions of GFM. These features include task lists (checkboxes), newlines corresponding to hard line breaks, auto-linked references to issues and commits, wiki links, and so on. To make matters more confusing, although task lists are not part of GFM proper, since 2014 they are rendered (in a read-only fashion) in all Markdown documents in repositories on the site.

These additional extensions are supported to varying degrees by Markdown Mode and GFM Mode as described below.

- **URL auto-linking**: Both Markdown Mode and GFM Mode support highlighting of URLs even without angle brackets.
- **Underscores inside words**: You must enable GFM Mode to toggle support for underscores inside of words. In this mode variable names such as `a_test_variable` will not trigger italics.
- **Fenced code blocks**: Code blocks between triple backquotes (```), with optional programming language keywords, are highlighted in both Markdown Mode and GFM Mode. They can be inserted with `C-c C-s C` (`markdown-insert-gfm-code-block`) or by typing three backquotes when `markdown-electric-backquote` is non-nil.
- **Strikethrough**: Strikethrough text is supported in both Markdown Mode and GFM Mode and can be inserted (and toggled) using `C-c C-s s` (`markdown-insert-strike-through`).
- **Task lists**: GFM task lists will be rendered as checkboxes, implemented using Emacs buttons, in both Markdown Mode and GFM Mode when `markdown-make-gfm-checkboxes-buttons` is set to a non-nil value (and this variable is `t` by default). These checkboxes can be toggled by clicking `mouse-1`, pressing `RET` over the button, or by pressing `C-c C-d` (`markdown-do`) with the point anywhere in the task list item. Alternatively, you can use the dedicated function `C-c C-x C-x` (`markdown-toggle-gfm-checkbox`) directly.
- **Wiki links**: Generic wiki links are supported in Markdown Mode, but in GFM Mode specifically they will be treated as they are on GitHub: spaces will be replaced by hyphens in file names and the first letter of the file name will be capitalized. For example, `[[wiki link]]` will map to a file named `Wiki-link` with the same extension as the current file.
- **Newlines**: Neither Markdown Mode nor GFM Mode does anything specifically with respect to newline behavior. If you use GFM Mode mostly to write text *for comments or issues* on the GitHub site—where newlines are indeed significant and correspond to hard line breaks—then you may want to enable `visual-line-mode` for line wrapping in buffers. You can do this with a `gfm-mode-hook` as follows:

```
;; Use visual-line-mode in gfm-mode
(defun my-gfm-mode-hook ()
  (visual-line-mode 1))
(add-hook 'gfm-mode-hook 'my-gfm-mode-hook)
```

- **Preview**: GFM-specific preview can be powered by setting `markdown-command` to use Docter (which, as of this writing, is unfortunately no longer maintained). This may also be configured to work with Marked 2 for `markdown-open-command`. See the Tips chapter for details.

* * *

5. Previewing & Exporting Files

There are a variety of ways to preview and export files in Markdown Mode. Perhaps the simplest way to quickly "preview" what your Markdown will look like on the web is to hide the markup in the buffer itself. Several other options are available which make use of an external Markdown processor (e.g., Markdown.pl, Pandoc, or MultiMarkdown). The various methods for previewing and exporting are summarized in the following table and described in more detail in the sections that follow.

Description	Keybinding	Destination/Viewer
Hide Markup	C-c C-x C-m	Same buffer
Compile	C-c C-c m	*markdown-output* buffer
Kill Ring Save	C-c C-c w	Kill ring
Preview	C-c C-c p	Browser (temporary file)
Export	C-c C-c e	<basename>.html
Export & View	C-c C-c v	<basename>.html, then browser
Live Preview	C-c C-c l	eww in an Emacs buffer
Open	C-c C-c o	markdown-open-command

All commands except Hide Markup and Open involve the additional step of sending the contents of the buffer to an external processor (`markdown-command`) to convert Markdown to HTML.

> To use Compile and other command commands that make use of an external Markdown processor, `markdown-command` must be configured as described in the Configuring Markdown section.

The Preview and Export commands are similar and worthy of more discussion. The difference is that when *previewing*, the output is written to a temporary file that is then opened in a browser. When *exporting*, the output is written to a file named like the one being visited, with the extension changed to .html instead, but the file is not opened. On the other hand, *viewing* is a combination of exporting and previewing: the file is saved permanently and then also opened for viewing.

> For the Export and View commands, the output file of form <basename>.html will be overwritten without notice.

The table above lists the keybindings for carrying out these commands, but they are also available from the Markdown menu when `menu-bar-mode` is enabled.

5.1 Markup Hiding

Markup hiding with `C-c C-x C-m` or `M-x markdown-toggle-markup-hiding` is one simple way to preview (and even edit) files. The side-by-side screenshots below illustrate the effects of this. Most markup will be hidden, including asterisks and underscores for italics and bold, square brackets and URLs for links, backquotes for inline code and fenced code blocks.

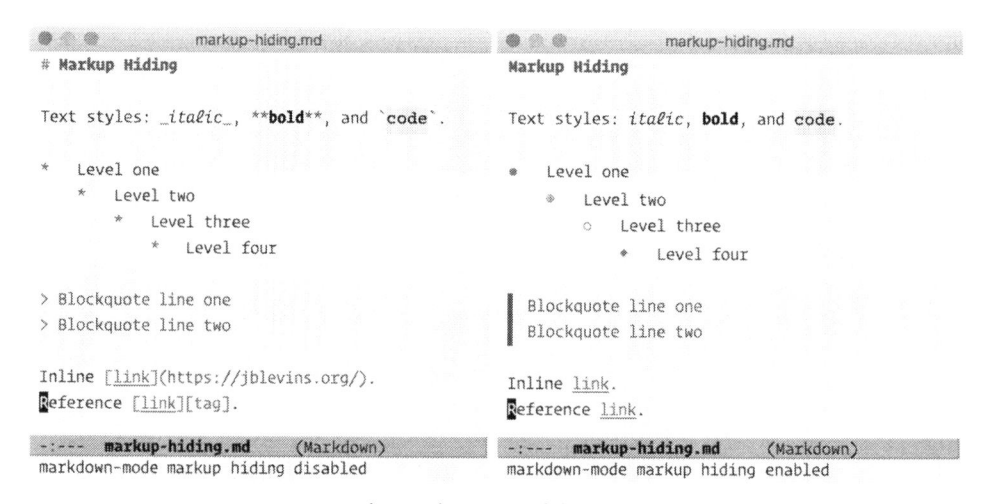

Markup Hiding in Markdown Mode

Note that markup hiding supersedes URL hiding. With markup hiding, the URL and surrounding markup is hidden entirely, while with URL hiding, only the URL itself is replaced by a composition character.

When Markup Hiding is enabled, the > prefix for blockquotes will be displayed as a special box drawing character. Horizontal rules, similarly, will be displayed using a line drawing character. List markers for unordered lists will be displayed using Unicode bullets, with different bullets for each level of nesting. Definition list markers, similarly, will be displayed using an alternative glyph. The alternative display characters can be changed by customizing the following variables.

`markdown-blockquote-display-char`
: String, default: 0x258C (left half block).[1]

    Character displayed when hiding blockquote markup.

`markdown-hr-display-char`
: Character, default: —.

    Character for hiding horizontal rule markup.

`markdown-definition-display-char`
: Character, default: 0x2058 (four dot punctuation).

    Character for replacing definition list markup.

`markdown-list-item-bullets`
: List of strings, default: 0x25cf (black circle), 0x25ce (bullseye), 0x25cb (white circle), 0x25c6 (black diamond), 0x25c7 (white diamond), 0x25ba (black right-pointing pointer), 0x2022 (bullet).

    List of bullets to use for unordered lists. It can contain any number of symbols, which will be repeated if nesting exceeds the list length.

> Markup hiding works by adding text properties to positions in the buffer—either the `invisible` property or the `display` property in cases where alternative glyphs are used (e.g., list bullets). *This does not, however, affect printing or other output.* Functions such as `htmlfontify-buffer` and `ps-print-buffer` will not honor these text properties. For printing, it would be better to convert to HTML or PDF first (e.g., using Pandoc) and then print.

5.2 Compiling to a Temporary Buffer or the Kill Ring

Compiling (i.e., running Markdown) with `C-c C-c m` (markdown-other-window) will send the contents of the current buffer to markdown-command and show the output in a temporary `*markdown-output*` buffer.

---

[1]Technical limitations prevent some characters from being displayed in the text. UTF-16 encodings and entity names are listed instead.

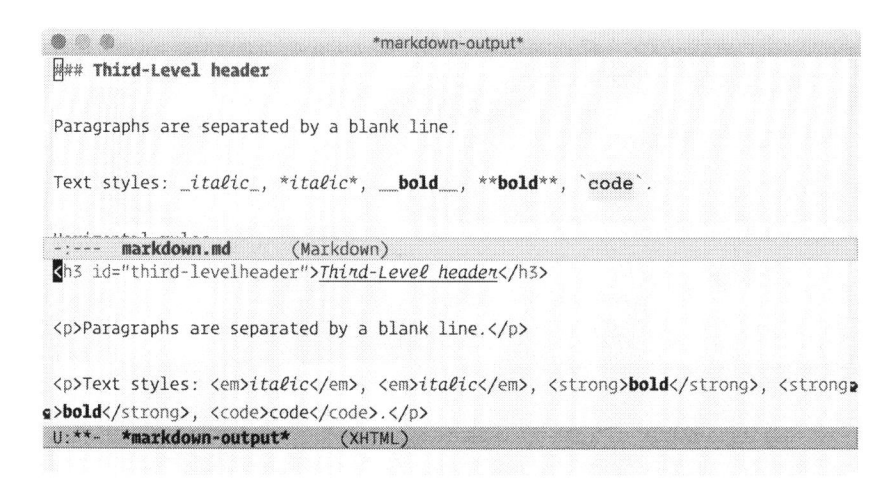

Markdown Output in a Separate Window

As an alternative, rather than displaying the output in another buffer you can save the output directly to the kill ring with C-c C-c w (markdown-kill-ring-save).

5.3 Static HTML Preview

Previewing the current buffer with C-c C-c p (markdown-preview) runs Markdown on the current buffer, stores the output in a temporary file, and opens or "previews" the file in the default browser.

> See the Tips chapter for details on how to configure the default browser in Emacs, and how to link to or include a custom stylesheet.

5.4 Static HTML Export & View

Exporting with C-c C-c e (markdown-export) will run Markdown (markdown-command) on the current buffer and save the result in the file <basename>.html, where <basename> is the name of the Markdown file visited by the current buffer, with the extension removed.

> As an example, if you are editing a file named notes.md, then the corresponding export file name would be notes.html.

Similarly *viewing* with `C-c C-c v` (`markdown-export-and-preview`) is the same as *exporting* the file and opening it in the default browser.

5.5 Live Preview Mode

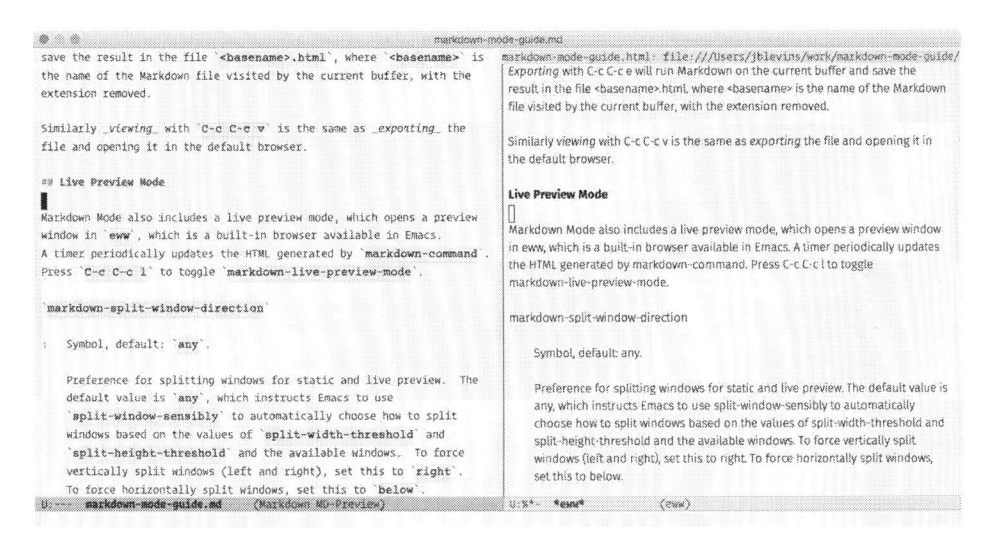

Live Preview Mode with the eww *Browser*

Markdown Mode also includes a live preview mode, which opens a preview window in eww, which is a built-in browser available in Emacs. An idle timer periodically refreshes the HTML generated by `markdown-command`. Press `C-c C-c l` to toggle `markdown-live-preview-mode`.

`markdown-split-window-direction`
> `any`, `right`, or `below`, default: any.

> Preference for splitting windows for static and live preview. The default value is any, which instructs Emacs to use `split-window-sensibly` to automatically choose how to split windows based on the values of `split-width-threshold` and `split-height-threshold` and the current window configuration. To force vertically split windows (left and right), set this to `right`. To force horizontally split windows, set this to `below`.

> *Example:*

```
(setq markdown-split-window-direction 'right)
```

markdown-live-preview-delete-export

nil, delete-on-export, or delete-on-destroy, default: delete-on-destroy.

Whether and when to delete the exported HTML file when using markdown-live-preview-export. If set to delete-on-export, delete on every export. When set to delete-on-destroy, delete when quitting markdown-live-preview-mode. If set to nil, never delete.

> For more complex configurations, markdown-live-preview-window-function can be customized to open in a browser other than eww.

5.6 Opening in a Standalone Markdown Previewer

A final option for previewing files is to use an external previewer with C-c C-c o (markdown-open). The program used to preview files is specified by the markdown-open-command variable, which must be customized to use an available external previewer on your system.

markdown-open-command

String, default: nil.

The command used for calling a standalone Markdown previewer capable of opening Markdown source files directly. This command will be called with a single argument, the file name of the current buffer.

Example:

```
(setq markdown-open-command "/usr/local/bin/mark")
```

> As described in the Tips chapter, one popular viewer on macOS is Marked 2, which can easily be used as with Markdown Mode with a simple shell script acting as a markdown-open-command wrapper.

5.7 Preview & Export Customization

`markdown-xhtml-standalone-regexp`

String, default: `"^\\(<\\?xml\\|<!DOCTYPE\\|<html\\)"`.

The regular expression that Markdown Mode uses to determine whether the output of `markdown-command` is a standalone HTML document or an HTML fragment. If this regular expression not matched in the first five lines of output, Markdown Mode assumes the output is a fragment and adds a header and footer.

`markdown-css-paths`

List of strings, default: `nil`.

A list of CSS files (URLs) to link to in the HTML output.

`markdown-content-type`

String, default: `""`.

When set to a nonempty string, an `http-equiv` attribute will be included in the HTML `<head>` block. If needed, the suggested values are `application/xhtml+xml` or `text/html`. See also: `markdown-coding-system`.

```
(setq markdown-content-type "application/xhtml+xml")
```

`markdown-coding-system`

String, default: `nil`.

Used for specifying the character set identifier in the `http-equiv` attribute when included. See `markdown-content-type`, which must be set before this variable has any effect. When set to `nil`, `buffer-file-coding-system` will be used to automatically determine the coding system string (falling back to `iso-8859-1` when unavailable). Common settings are `utf-8` and `iso-latin-1`.

Example:

```
(setq markdown-coding-system "utf-8")
```

`markdown-xhtml-header-content`

String, default: `""`.

Additional content to include in the HTML `<head>` block.

Example:

```
(setq markdown-xhtml-header-content
      (concat "<link rel=\"shortcut icon\""
              " href=\"/favicon.ico\""
              " type=\"image/png\"/>"))
```

`markdown-before-export-hook`

List of functions, default: `nil`.

Hook run before running `markdown-command` to export HTML output. The hook may modify the buffer, which will be restored to the original state after exporting is complete.

`markdown-after-export-hook`

List of functions, default: `nil`.

Hook run after HTML output has been saved. Any changes to the output buffer made by this hook will be saved.

* * *

6. Tips

This chapter contains additional tips about using Markdown Mode and integration with other third-party packages.

6.1 Using Markdown Mode with Other File Extensions

Markdown Mode contains `autoload` statements to automatically associate itself with `.md` and `.markdown` files in `auto-mode-alist`. If you use another file extension for your Markdown files, say `.text`, then you can also ask Emacs to load `markdown-mode` automatically for `.text` files by adding the following to your init file:

```
(add-to-list 'auto-mode-alist '("\\.text\\'" . markdown-mode))
```

Alternatively, if you load packages with `use-package`, you can achieve the same thing using the `:mode` keyword, like so:

```
(use-package markdown-mode
  :mode (("\\.text\\'" . markdown-mode)))
```

> This is a macro and after expanding it with `pp-macroexpand-last-sexp` we see that it is equivalent to auto-loading `markdown-mode` and updating `auto-mode-alist`:
>
> ```
> (progn
>   (unless
>       (fboundp 'markdown-mode)
>     (autoload #'markdown-mode "markdown-mode" nil t))
>   (ignore
>    (add-to-list 'auto-mode-alist
>                 '("\\.text\\'" . markdown-mode))))
> ```

6.2 Switching and Toggling Markup

There are a couple of ways to quickly switch or toggle markup in Markdown Mode (e.g., from bold to italic). As an example, suppose you type `**italic**` and want to change it to `*italic*`. You can quickly fix the mistake in at least two ways.

1. **Using the kill ring**: Move the point to the erroneously bold word and press `C-c C-k` (`markdown-kill-thing-at-point`). This removes the bold text and adds "italic", without the asterisks, to the kill ring. Then press `C-c C-s i` to insert an empty italic span and yank in the "italic" text with `C-y`.
2. **Using markup toggling**: Markdown Mode allows you to "toggle" certain markup, including that for bold, italic, and inline code, by repeating the insertion command. Returning to the example, you can press `C-c C-s b` to first remove (toggle) the bold asterisks, leaving only "italic" behind. Then, pressing `C-c C-s i` surrounds the word with single asterisks.

These methods also apply to other forms of markup such as inline code and even links.

You can also toggle between asterisks and underscores as needed. Suppose that you have `__bold__` in the buffer and want to use asterisks instead. Both will render in HTML as bold, but you might have a preference for the latter in plain text. You can use the Markdown Mode cycling commands to switch between underscores and asterisks in bold and italic phrases by pressing either `C-c C--` or `C-c C-=` (`markdown-promote` or `markdown-demote`).

6.3 Linking to or Including Custom CSS

The default stylesheet for HTML in most browsers is rather plain by design, so you may want to use a custom stylesheet by either linking to an external stylesheet or including a `<style>` block in the exported HTML itself.

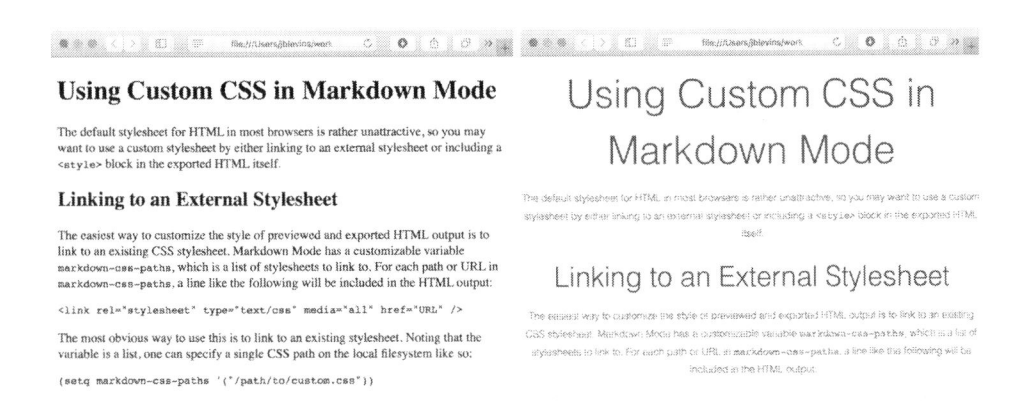

Default and Custom CSS in Markdown Mode Output

Linking to an External Stylesheet

The easiest way to customize the style of previewed and exported HTML output is to link to an existing CSS stylesheet. Markdown Mode has a customizable variable `markdown-css-paths`, which is a list of stylesheets to link to. For each path or URL in `markdown-css-paths`, a line like the following will be included in the HTML output:

```
<link rel="stylesheet" type="text/css" media="all" href="URL" />
```

Noting that the variable is a list, one can specify a single CSS path on the local filesystem like so:

```
(setq markdown-css-paths '("/path/to/custom.css"))
```

On the other hand, to link to an existing URL you can use the following form:

```
(setq markdown-css-paths '("http://mydomain.com/style.css"))
```

As another example, the Marked 2 previewer contains several built-in stylesheets that users can choose between. Conveniently, these stylesheets are stored on the filesystem as CSS files inside the application package and you can link to them locally. To use the "Lopash" style when previewing from `markdown-mode`, you can set the `markdown-css-paths` list as follows:

```
(setq markdown-css-paths
    '("/Applications/Marked 2.app/Contents/Resources/Lopash.css"))
```

If you don't have a stylesheet already, there are many popular Markdown stylesheets available online. For example, here are three such repositories on GitHub:

- http://markdowncss.github.io
- http://jasonm23.github.io/markdown-css-themes/
- https://sindresorhus.com/github-markdown-css/

Embedding a Custom Stylesheet

As an alternative to linking to an external stylesheet, you can also include inline style information in output files by using the `markdown-xhtml-header-content` variable. This variable specifies a string to add to the `<head>` block of the HTML output.

> For example, to remove the default underline property from links, but temporarily underline links when hovering, you can include the following `<style>` block via `markdown-xhtml-header-content`:
>
> ```
> (setq markdown-xhtml-header-content
>       "<style type='text/css'>
> a { text-decoration: none; }
> a:hover { text-decoration: underline; }
> </style>")
> ```

> For more advanced customization, there are two export hooks available: `markdown-before-export-hook` and `markdown-after-export-hook`.

6.4 Imenu and Imenu-List

Markdown Mode includes support for `imenu`, an interface for quickly navigating to different sections within a buffer. To try `imenu` with Markdown Mode, simply run `M-x imenu-add-menubar-index`. An "Index" menu will appear in the menubar. Clicking a heading moves the point to that heading. Alternatively, when invoking `M-x imenu` using the keyboard Emacs will present you with a list of headings in the minibuffer.

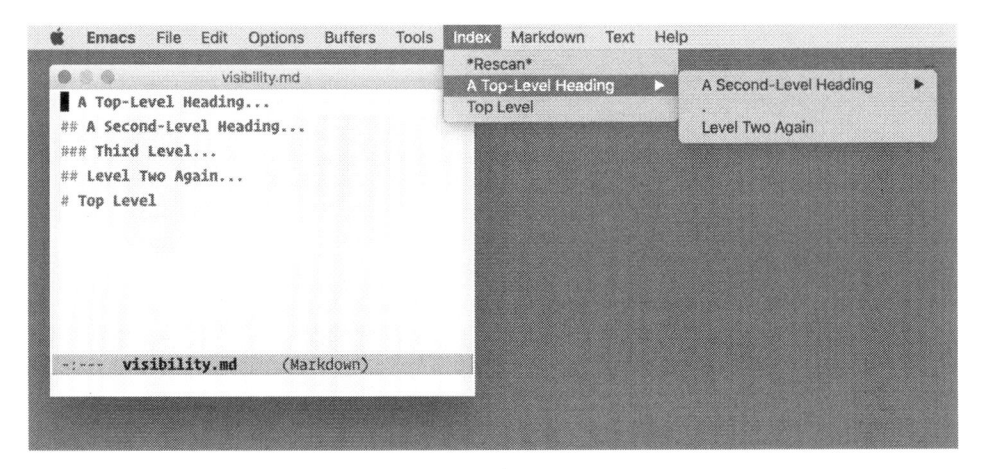

imenu Index Menu

Markdown Mode adds a single period (.) to the top of each sub-menu. Clicking it takes you to the parent section. Otherwise, there is no way to jump directly to headings that are not leaf nodes in the heading tree.

To automatically load `imenu` when `markdown-mode` is loaded, you can add the following to your `.emacs` or `init.el` file:

```
(add-hook 'markdown-mode-hook 'imenu-add-menubar-index)
(setq imenu-auto-rescan t)
```

The first line asks Emacs to run the `imenu-add-menubar-index` function each time markdown-mode is loaded. The second line asks `imenu` to keep the index up to date when files are modified, as sections are added or removed.

By default, the `imenu` menu is nested. If you prefer a flat menu, you can customize `markdown-nested-imenu-heading-index`.

`markdown-nested-imenu-header-index`
> Boolean, default: `t`.
>
> Use nested `imenu` heading index when non-`nil` and a flat menu otherwise. A nested index may provide more natural browsing from the menu bar, but a flat list may allow for faster keyboard navigation via tab completion.

Another useful `imenu`-based package is `imenu-list`, a third-party package which shows the current buffer's `imenu` entries in a pop-up buffer. You can install `imenu-list` from MELPA. With use-package, you can configure it like so:

```
(use-package imenu-list
  :ensure t
  :bind (("C-'" . imenu-list-smart-toggle))
  :config
  (setq imenu-list-focus-after-activation t
        imenu-list-auto-resize nil))
```

This binds `C-'` (`imenu-list-smart-toggle`) so that when pressing it a window appears on the right side showing the heading hierarchy in the `*Ilist*` buffer. Pressing `C-'` again hides the window.

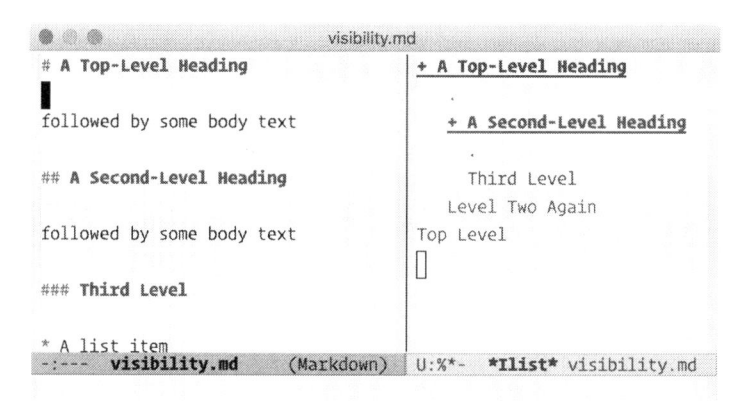

Markdown Mode with `imenu-list`

By default, the point stays in the original window and so the `*Ilist*` window is not focused. Setting the variable `imenu-list-focus-after-activation` to a non-`nil` value, as above, changes the focus to the new window so that you can immediately issue commands there.

The `*Ilist*` buffer is periodically refreshed. If you want the width of the window containing it to adjust automatically each time it is refreshed, then set the variable `imenu-list-auto-resize` to `t` instead.

There are several keybindings in the `*Ilist*` buffer for navigating between sections:

- RET or mouse click - visit heading at point

- `SPC` - visit heading, but keep focus on `*Ilist*` buffer
- `TAB` or `f` - fold/unfold subtree
- `n` and `p` - next/previous line
- `g` - refresh entries
- `q` - quit window and disable `imenu-list-minor-mode`

Unlike the `imenu` Index menu, the `*Ilist*` buffer is updated automatically.

6.5 File Local Variables

Emacs allows one to specify values for variables inside files themselves. For example, you can specify which mode Emacs should use to edit a particular file by setting a special variable named `mode`. You can specify such file local variables at either the beginning or end of a file.

Perhaps you have seen lines like the following at the beginning of scripts. This particular line tells Emacs that you would like to open this file using `cperl-mode`:

```
#!/usr/bin/perl          -*- mode: cperl -*-
```

The `mode` variable is special; it is not an actual variable name in Emacs. Another special variable is `coding`, which specifies the character coding system for this file (e.g., `utf-8` or `latin-1`). A third special variable is `eval`, which specifies a Lisp expression to evaluate. Multiple `eval` declarations can be given in the same file.

Among the special variables, `mode` is the most special of all and so the `mode:` declaration can even be omitted:

```
#!/usr/bin/perl          -*-cperl-*-
```

File variable definitions should appear in a comment and the comment syntax used by Markdown Mode is the same as for HTML comments: `<!-- comment -->`. So, to specify a local variable at the beginning of a file you could add the following to the first line (which would result in Emacs loading the file in `gfm-mode` instead of, say, `markdown-mode`):

```
<!-- -*- mode: gfm -*- -->
```

To specify multiple variables, separate them by semicolons:

```
<!-- -*- mode: markdown; coding: utf-8 -*- -->
```

Alternatively, you can insert a local variable block at the *end* of a file. Such a block opens with a `Local Variables:` declaration and closes with `End:`, like so:

```
<!-- Local Variables: -->
<!-- markdown-enable-math: t -->
<!-- End: -->
```

It is not necessary that each line is a self-contained comment, so the following also works and it is a personal preference which form you use:

```
<!--
Local Variables:
markdown-enable-math: t
End:
-->
```

One useful scenario for using file local variables with Markdown files include toggling special modes, like setting `markdown-enable-math` in the previous example. If you mostly leave math mode disabled (so that $ is not a special character), but sometimes want to enable it, using a file-local variable as above is a great way to handle this case.

Other example uses are setting the `fill-column` in a particular file, or declaring that spaces should be used for indentation instead of tabs:

```
<!--
Local Variables:
fill-column: 70
indent-tabs-mode: nil
End:
-->
```

6.6 Generating a Table of Contents

A package called `markdown-toc` allows users to generate and update a table of contents in Markdown files. Like Markdown Mode itself, you can install it from MELPA or MELPA Stable: `M-x package-install RET markdown-toc`.

To insert the table of contents initially, place the point where you would like it to appear and issue M-x markdown-toc-generate-toc. You will see a header comment, a title, a Markdown-formatted nested list of headings, and a footer comment, as in the following example:

```
<!-- markdown-toc start - Don't edit this section.
     Run M-x markdown-toc-generate-toc again -->
**Table of Contents**

- [Introduction](#introduction)
    - [Quick Reference](#quick-reference)
    - [Markdown](#markdown)
        - [Markdown Syntax Reference](#markdown-syntax-reference)
        - [Additional Information](#additional-information)
    ...

<!-- markdown-toc end -->
```

After it has been inserted, you can update the table of contents with M-x markdown-toc-refresh-toc. As an alternative, you can use the combined generate-or-refresh command M-x markdown-toc-generate-or-refresh-toc. Finally, to remove it run M-x markdown-toc-delete-toc.

> Notice that markdown-toc generates anchors (e.g., #quick-reference) automatically. You will need to make sure that your Markdown processor of choice also generates these in the resulting HTML and that it follows the same format (i.e., replacing spaces with hyphens). This is the format used by MultiMarkdown, for example.

You can also customize the title and the start and end comments:

```
(custom-set-variables
 '(markdown-toc-header-toc-start "<!-- customized start-->")
 '(markdown-toc-header-toc-title "**customized title**")
 '(markdown-toc-header-toc-end "<!-- customized end -->"))
```

6.7 Highlighting and Preserving Whitespace

Whitespace is an important part of Markdown. For example, two spaces at the end of a line produce a hard line break and blocks indented by four spaces become code blocks.

If you want to temporarily display whitespace in a file, you can enable `whitespace-mode`, which is part of Emacs, by typing `M-x whitespace-mode`. Issue the command again to disable it.

On a related note, if you use `whitespace-cleanup-mode` to tidy up your files automatically, then you may want to disable it in `markdown-mode`. To do so, you can add the following to your init file:

```
(after-load 'whitespace-cleanup-mode
            (push 'markdown-mode whitespace-cleanup-mode-ignore-modes))
```

6.8 Using Flyspell with Markdown Mode

Flyspell Mode enables on-the-fly spell checking in Emacs. If you want to always enable `flyspell-mode` when Markdown Mode is loaded, you can add the following to your init file:

```
(add-hook 'markdown-mode-hook 'flyspell-mode)
```

Starting with version 2.3, Markdown Mode defines a `flyspell-generic-check-word-predicate` function which lets Flyspell know that it should ignore code blocks, inline code, and comments, reference labels, Markdown markup, and URLs.

6.9 Keeping Notes in a Local Wiki

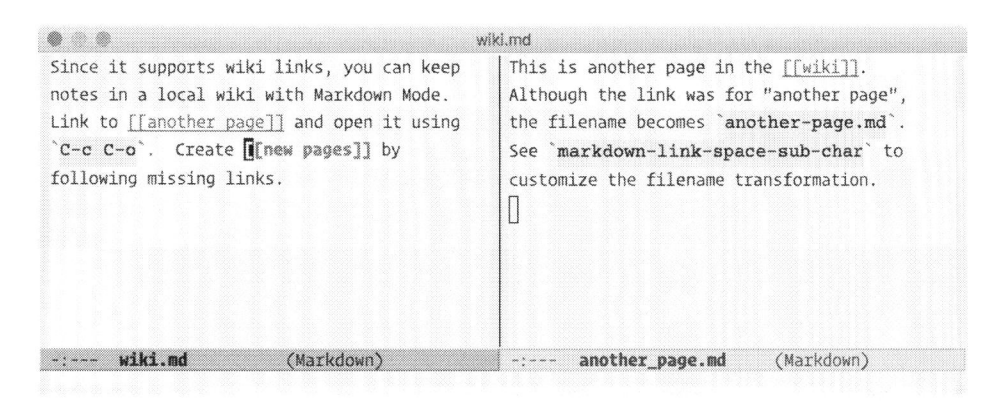

Local Wiki Files in Markdown Mode

Markdown Mode supports wiki links, so you can use it keep notes in a local wiki. You can create [[wiki links]] to other files and open them by moving the point to the link and pressing C-c C-o. If a file doesn't exist, it will be created. You can move quickly between links with M-n (markdown-next-link) and M-p (markdown-previous-link).

As discussed in the section on Wiki Links, there are several settings you may want to customize. When following wiki links, Markdown Mode looks for a file with the same extension as the current one. The variable markdown-link-space-sub-char determines how spaces are handled when transforming the link text to a file name. Finally, if you want to highlight missing links as in the screenshot above, set markdown-wiki-link-fontify-missing to t.

6.10 Integration with Deft Mode

Deft Mode with Notes in Markdown Format

Deft is an Emacs mode for quickly browsing, filtering, and editing directories of plain text notes, inspired by Notational Velocity. It was designed for increased productivity when writing and taking notes by making it fast and simple to find the right file at the right time and by automating many of the usual tasks such as creating new files and saving files.

If you keep notes in Markdown format (perhaps in wiki form, as in the previous section), then you might also enjoy Deft. You don't have to use Markdown—Deft works with LaTeX files, Org files, etc.—but it has some Markdown-specific features. For example, it automatically strips Markdown heading markup when displaying note titles. It also allows you to customize the Markdown heading level of new notes.

Below is a simplified version of my own Deft configuration, which I mostly use with Markdown files. This binds Deft to `<f8>`, enables recursive subdirectory search for notes, configures several file extensions I use for notes, and customizes some of the file naming and titling options.

```
(use-package deft
  :bind (("<f8>" . deft))
  :commands (deft deft-open-file deft-new-file-named)
  :config
  (setq deft-directory "~/notes/"
        deft-recursive t
        deft-extensions '("md" "txt" "org" "tex")
        deft-use-filter-string-for-filename nil
        deft-use-filename-as-title nil
        deft-markdown-mode-title-level 1
        deft-file-naming-rules '((noslash . "-")
                                 (nospace . "-")
                                 (case-fn . downcase))))
```

6.11 MathJax Integration

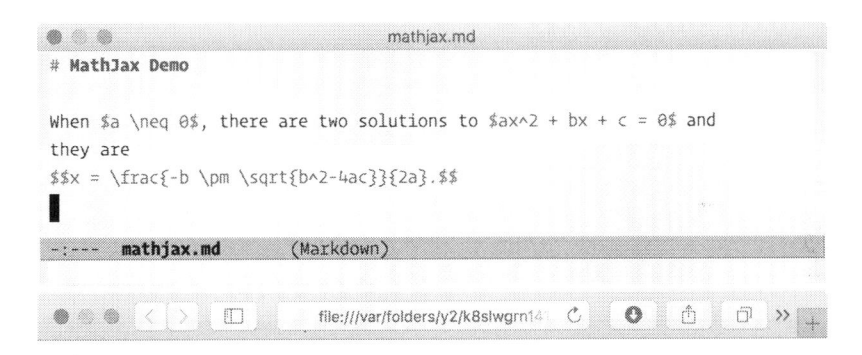

Markdown with Math Mode and MathJax Preview

If you want to include mathematical expressions in LaTeX form in your Markdown files, Markdown Mode assists you with Math Mode for editing (see the Extensions chapter for details). For viewing or publishing, you will need some way to view the LaTeX in a readable form. One option is to use MathJax, a cross-browser JavaScript package for rendering mathematics in LaTeX and MathML form.

Even if you don't use MathJax in your publication workflow, it can be useful for previewing Markdown files containing mathematics. To do this, you can ask Markdown Mode to add the necessary JavaScript tags to the `<head>` block of your HTML preview output using the `markdown-xhtml-header-content` variable:

```
(setq markdown-xhtml-header-content
      (concat "<script type=\"text/javascript\" async"
              " src=\"https://cdnjs.cloudflare.com/ajax/libs/mathjax/"
              "2.7.1/MathJax.js?config=TeX-MML-AM_CHTML\">"
              "</script>"))
```

> ⚠ The `TeX-MML-AM_CHTML` configuration in the example above very general, and therefore larger than other configurations. It is useful as a default to get started, but you will most likely want to use a more appropriate, specific configuration for production use, for better performance.

> ⚠ You will need to make sure that your Markdown processor is generating HTML fragments, rather than standalone documents, so that Markdown Mode can add a header and footer with your custom `<script>` tag.

6.12 Using Pre- and Post-Processors

A Unix "pipeline" is a sequence of processes connected through *pipes*. The standard output of each process is directed to the standard input of the following one.

> ✎ To give a generic example of pipes, the following command lists all running processes, filters out those without `markdown` in the name, removes the `grep markdown` process itself, extracts the process IDs using `awk`:
>
> ```
> ps aux | grep markdown | grep -v grep | awk '{print $2}'
> ```

With Markdown Mode, the Markdown processor given by the variable `markdown-command` can be a pipeline, and so it can be used to apply pre- or post-processors to your Markdown files.

As an example, one common Markdown post-processor is SmartyPants, which implements "smart typography" (curly quotation marks, en-dashes, em-dashes, and so on). To use it, you will need to first install SmartyPants.

- On Debian Linux, you can install `libtext-typography-perl`.
- On macOS with Homebrew, you can use `brew install smartypants`.
- Otherwise, you can install it manually by downloading the SmartyPants zip file, uncompressing it, and placing `SmartyPants.pl` in your `PATH`.

Once you have SmartyPants installed, note the path of the script. For example, suppose it is installed in your Emacs `exec-path` path as `smartypants`. Then to use SmartyPants when previewing and exporting from Markdown Mode, you would set `markdown-command` so that the `markdown` output is piped to `smartypants`. You can do this either by using `M-x customize-group RET markdown` or by placing the following in your init file:

```
(setq markdown-command "markdown | smartypants")
```

6.13 Using a Custom Web Browser

To open a browser, Markdown Mode calls the function specified in `browse-url-browser-function`. To determine what value is currently used in your own Emacs, you can use `M-x describe-variable RET browse-url-browser-function`. To use a different browser, customize the variable with `M-x customize-option RET browse-url-browser-function` and answer the questions presented.

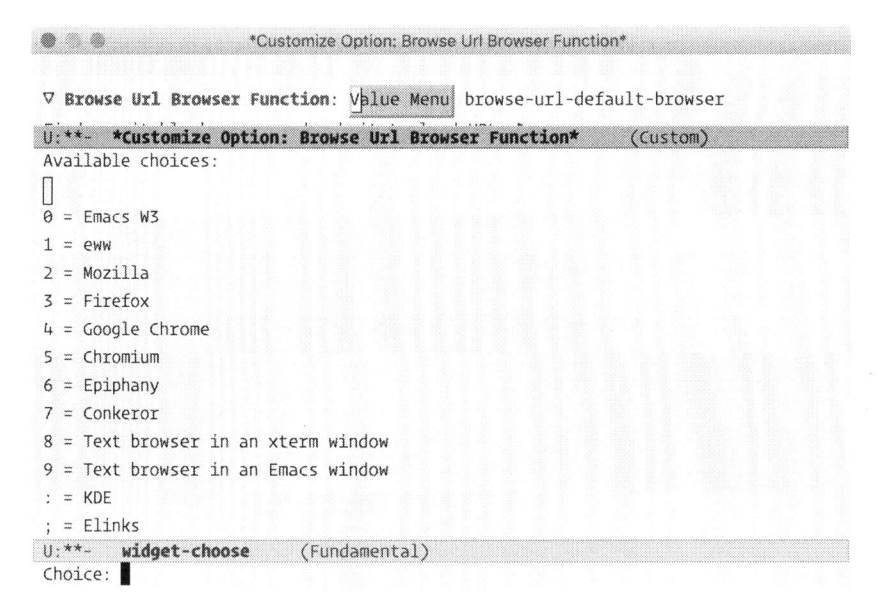

Customizing `browse-url-browser-function`

If you want to change the setting in your init file instead, you can simply add something like the following:

```
(setq browse-url-browser-function #'browse-url-chrome)
```

For reference, here is a selection of the available `browse-url` functions in Emacs 25.2:

```
browse-url-chrome                    browse-url-epiphany
browse-url-chromium                  browse-url-firefox
browse-url-conkeror                  browse-url-galeon
browse-url-default-browser           browse-url-generic
browse-url-default-macosx-browser    browse-url-gnome-moz
browse-url-default-windows-browser   browse-url-kde
browse-url-elinks                    browse-url-mozilla
browse-url-elinks-new-window         browse-url-w3
```

If your browser is not supported, choose `browse-url-generic` and set `browse-url-generic-program` to the path of your browser's executable. The downside of using a generic browser is that you lose "remote control" and as a result, a new process will be spawned for every URL you open.

The above options change the browser for Emacs *globally*. On the other hand, if for some reason you only wanted to change the browser used for Markdown Mode previewing specifically, you can achieve this by "advising" the `markdown-preview` function:

```
(advice-add 'markdown-preview :around
            (lambda (orig &rest args)
              "Use Chromium as default browser."
              (let ((browse-url-browser-function #'browse-url-chromium))
                (apply orig args))))
```

This example changes the browse function to `browse-url-chromium` for the `markdown-preview` function only. See the section on Advising Emacs Lisp Functions in the Emacs Lisp Reference Manual for additional details.

6.14 Using Marked 2 as a Standalone Previewer

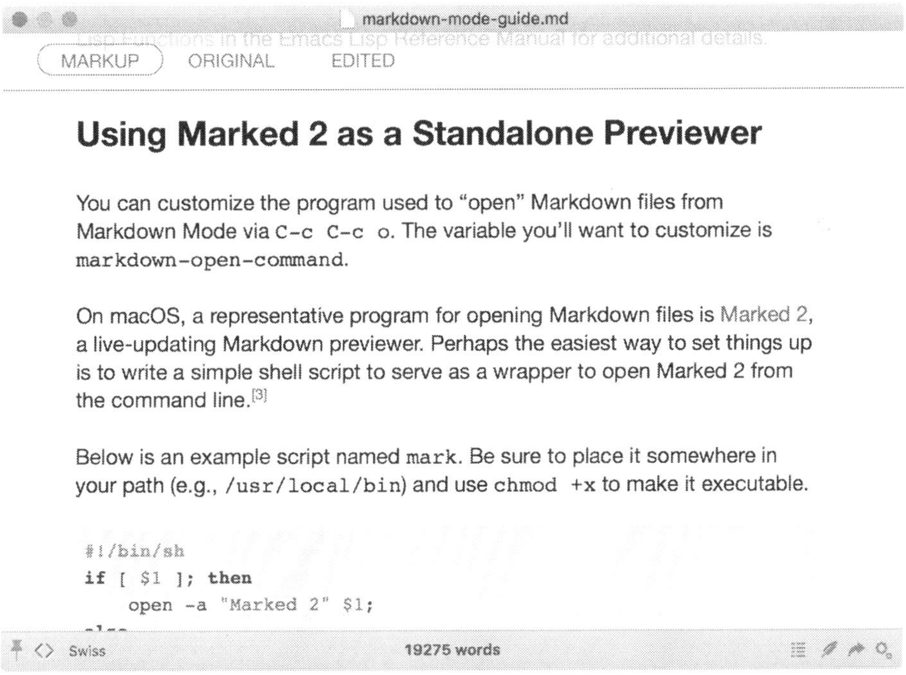

Marked 2 Preview of this Book

You can customize the program used to "open" Markdown files from Markdown Mode via `C-c C-c o`. The variable you will want to customize is `markdown-open-command`.

On macOS, a popular application for opening Markdown files is Marked 2, a live-updating Markdown previewer. Perhaps the easiest way to configure Markdown Mode to use it is to write a simple shell script to serve as a wrapper to open Marked 2 from the command line.[1]

Below is an example script named `mark`. Be sure to place it somewhere in your path (e.g., `/usr/local/bin`) and use `chmod +x` to make it executable.

Shell Script to Use Marked 2 as a Previewer

```sh
#!/bin/sh
if [ $1 ]; then
    open -a "Marked 2" $1;
else
    open -a "Marked 2";
fi
```

Then you can ask Markdown Mode to call the script for opening the current file by setting `markdown-open-command`:

```
(setq markdown-open-command "/usr/local/bin/mark")
```

Furthermore, once you install the `mark` script you can simply type `mark <filename>` in a terminal to open a Markdown file.

6.15 Pandoc Mode

Pandoc, in addition to being a Markdown-to-HTML processor, can convert multiple input formats to each of several output formats. For example, it can also convert Markdown to LaTeX or Org format.

Pandoc Mode is an Emacs interface for Pandoc, implemented as a minor mode. You can install it from MELPA or MELPA Stable and activate it by typing `M-x pandoc-mode`. The documentation summarizes Pandoc Mode as follows:

---

[1] See https://jblevins.org/log/marked-2-command for details.

pandoc-mode uses the hydra package to create a keyboard-driven menu interface to all options and settings. Pressing C-c / calls the main menu. After that, everything should be self-explanatory. From the main menu, you can run pandoc on the buffer, view the output buffer and the current settings, set the input and output formats, and you can go to the options menu.

Some examples of settings Pandoc Mode can manage for you are:

- produce standalone output or a snippet,
- use a template file,
- generate a table of contents,
- include a header or footer,
- set the syntax highlighting style,
- render mathematical equations,
- link to a CSS stylesheet.

These are but a few of the available options. Pandoc Mode also adds font lock support for Pandoc citations and numbered example lists.

With Pandoc Mode you can create multiple output profiles for a single input file. You might have a Markdown file that you want to convert to HTML for publishing on your website and to PDF for printing.

You can change the output settings from the pandoc-mode menus, or you can store them in settings files on a per-project or global basis. If your main file name is article.md then the settings file for HTML output would be .article.md.html.pandoc.

If you use Pandoc Mode often, you can add a hook to load it automatically with Markdown Mode whenever a pandoc-mode settings file is detected:

```
(add-hook 'markdown-mode-hook 'conditionally-turn-on-pandoc)
```

6.16 R Markdown

R Markdown is a Markdown dialect created by RStudio specifically for producing reports from the R statistical package. For example, it supports evaluation of R code blocks, with the output of the code included in the document. R Markdown supports a variety of output formats, including HTML, PDF, and Word.

R Markdown files have the .Rmd extension, so at the very least you will want to use markdown-mode for those files. For example:

```
(add-to-list 'auto-mode-alist '("\\.Rmd\\'" . markdown-mode))
```

The basic Markdown syntax is unchanged in R Markdown, but it supports several extensions. Fenced code blocks with braces around the language name are used to format R code blocks:

```
```{r}
summary(cars$dist)
summary(cars$speed)
```
```

You can also provide options in the code block info string:

```
```{r, eval=FALSE}
summary(cars)
```
```

Markdown Mode will use `r-mode` for syntax highlighting in these code blocks if you enable native font lock. To do so, use `markdown-toggle-fontify-code-blocks-natively` or `C-c C-x C-f`.

6.17 Tracking Changes with CriticMarkup Mode

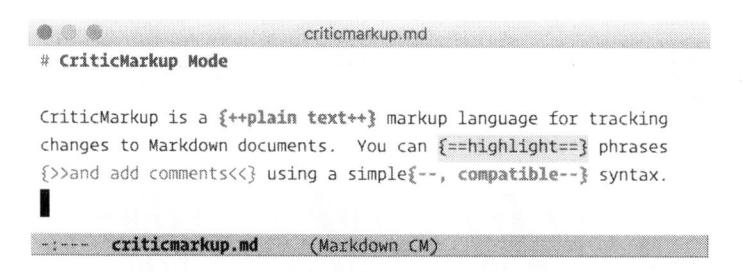

CriticMarkup Mode and Markdown Mode

CriticMarkup is a plain text markup language for tracking changes to Markdown and other compatible documents. It defines the following tags for marking changes:

- Addition: `{++added++}`

- Deletion: {--removed--}
- Substitution: {~~old~>new~~}
- Comment: {>>comment<<}
- Highlight: {==highlight==}{>>comment<<}

cm-mode is a minor mode that provides support for CriticMarkup in Emacs. Like other packages described, it is available on MELPA and MELPA Stable. First, it provides font-lock support for the markup tags above, and it defines the customizable faces used to highlight them. To customize the faces, see the `criticmarkup-faces` group. Second, it provides keybindings for insert CriticMarkup tags to track changes in a file:

- C-c * a - add text
- C-c * d - delete text
- C-c * s - substitute text
- C-c * c - insert a comment (possibly with highlight)

cm-mode uses C-c * as a prefix, but this can easily be changed to, say, C-c c like so:

```
(define-key cm-mode-map (kbd "C-c *") nil)
(define-key cm-mode-map (kbd "C-c c") cm-prefix-map)
```

6.18 Editing HTML as Markdown

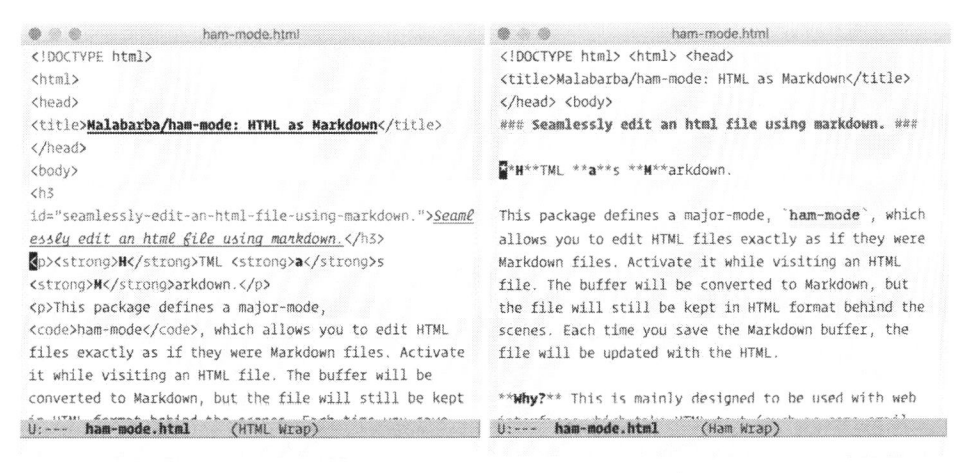

HTML Mode and HTML as Markdown Mode

HTML as Markdown Mode, or `ham-mode`, allows you to edit HTML files as if they were Markdown files. That is, it provides a transparent layer so that you can edit an HTML file using Markdown Mode. It first converts the HTML to Markdown but any updates to the contents are converted back to HTML.

To install the package from MELPA or MELPA Stable, simply run `M-x package-install RET ham-mode`. To activate it while visiting an HTML file, run `M-x ham-mode`.

6.19 Editing Markdown Tables with Org Table Mode

Although there is no official table syntax in Markdown, a couple of widely accepted table formats have emerged. Implementing a full-featured table editing mode, such as `orgtbl-mode` in Org Mode, would require tremendous effort, and so unfortunately Markdown Mode does not yet support table editing. However, with a little work, and if one is brave enough, `orgtbl-mode` can be adapted to help in editing basic Markdown tables.

Here, we consider the pipe table syntax of PHP Markdown Extra because of its similarity to Org Mode tables.

```
| First Header  | Second Header |
|---------------|---------------|
| Content Cell  | Content Cell  |
| Content Cell  | Content Cell  |
```

This is a rather simple table, but notably the only difference with the Org table counterpart is the point at which the lines cross in the center. Instead of -|-, Org uses -+-:

```
| First Header  | Second Header |
|---------------+---------------|
| Content Cell  | Content Cell  |
| Content Cell  | Content Cell  |
```

If you toggle on `orgtbl-mode`, it will recognize either table, but when you re-align with `C-c C-c`, the result will be converted to Org format, which will not be rendered correctly by Markdown processors. One way around this—which to be clear is a hack and is not recommended for important work—is to *advise* the `orgtbl-mode` alignment function so that at the end it converts the intersections back to Markdown pipe table form.

The following function temporarily narrows the buffer to the table in question and replaces instances of `-+-` with `-|-`. It only does so in `markdown-mode` or `gfm-mode`, so as not to disturb actual Org tables.

```
(require 'org-table)

(defun markdown-org-table-align-advice ()
  "Replace \"+\" sign with \"|\" in tables."
  (when (member major-mode '(markdown-mode gfm-mode))
    (save-excursion
      (save-restriction
        (narrow-to-region (org-table-begin) (org-table-end))
        (goto-char (point-min))
        (while (search-forward "-+-" nil t)
          (replace-match "-|-"))))))

(advice-add 'org-table-align :after 'markdown-org-table-align-advice)
```

Once this code is evaluated, when you run `org-table-align`, such as when pressing C-c C-c, the table will be automatically converted back to Markdown format.

> ⚠ This simple function does not handle the full syntax, such as indicators for table alignment, but it may be useful as a starting point for more robust versions.

* * *

7. Markdown Mode Development

Markdown Mode is an open source project. The primary repository for Markdown Mode is on GitHub. Anyone can easily browse the project files by visiting the project's GitHub page at https://github.com/jrblevin/markdown-mode.

If you would like to contribute to Markdown Mode development, the best way to start is to clone the Git repository. You can clone the repository using the HTTPS, SSH, and Git protocols:

```
git clone https://github.com/jrblevin/markdown-mode.git
git clone git://github.com/jrblevin/markdown-mode.git
git clone ssh://git@github.com:jrblevin/markdown-mode.git
```

7.1 Testing the Development Version

To test the current development version, you may either download `markdown-mode.el` from the GitHub repository or install the `markdown-mode` package from MELPA.

Note that by nature, the development version of Markdown Mode may be unstable or even unusable at times. It is not recommend for daily use unless you are fine with things occasionally breaking. Function names, features, keybindings, etc. may change without notice.

Supposing you have stored `markdown-mode.el` in directory named `/path/to/markdown-mode`, then you will probably need to make sure that Emacs can find it by adding something like the following to your init file:

```
(add-to-list 'load-path "/path/to/markdown-mode")
```

Alternatively, you can install the `markdown-mode` package from the (unstable) MELPA repository. In this case, you might need to tell the package manager about the repository in your init file, like so:

```
(require 'package)
(add-to-list 'package-archives
             '("melpa" . "http://melpa.org/packages/"))
(package-initialize)
```

7.2 Reporting Bugs and Issues

Markdown Mode is developed and tested primarily for compatibility with GNU Emacs 24.3 and later. If you are using an older version of Emacs, please update to a more recent version first to see if the issue persists.

If you do find a bug in Markdown Mode, please construct a test case—and if possible a patch—and open a ticket on the GitHub issue tracker at https://github.com/jrblevin/markdown-mode/issues. Before reporting an issue, please try to reproduce the issue with a minimal Emacs configuration, for example, by starting Emacs without your usual local init file (e.g., starting with `emacs --no-init`) and then loading `markdown-mode` with `M-x load-file`.

7.3 Submitting Patches or GitHub Pull Requests

Below are some guidelines for submitting patches. Ideally, these should be submitted in the form of GitHub pull requests, but email patches are also fine if that is more convenient. For pull requests, it is recommended to create a new feature branch (e.g., `feat/my-new-feature`) and submit the pull request from that branch. (If you instead add commits to the `master` branch in your own repository, it's more difficult to get back in sync if changes are required to the patch.)

- Markdown mode contributions should adhere to both the GNU Emacs Lisp coding conventions and the Major Mode Conventions.
- Test cases are needed for significant changes. Markdown Mode uses the `ert` (Emacs Lisp Regression Testing) library. If you are not familiar with writing tests, there are hundreds of examples in `markdown-test.el` that you can use as a starting point for new tests.
- You can confirm that your tests pass by either typing `make test` from the command line or by issuing a GitHub pull request and letting the Travis CI integration on GitHub run the tests for you.
- Please be sure to update the documentation at the top of `markdown-mode.el` and the docstrings for related variables or functions.

- If your patch involves changes to the documentation, you can update the README.md file by running the webpage.sh script.
- Finally, it's also helpful if you update the CHANGES.md file to reflect the bug you fixed or the feature you added or improved.

* * *

8. Conclusion

8.1 Looking Back and Looking Ahead

When I wrote the first version of `markdown-mode.el` over ten years ago, I never imagined it would reach as many people as it has. This was before GitHub was founded and around the same time `package.el` was initially being developed. Emacs 21.4 was the latest release and Markdown itself was three years old.

Markdown Mode development continues and my goals for upcoming releases are to improve performance, streamline the code base, build a more robust Markdown parsing engine, and make it easier for users to choose feature sets to match their preferred Markdown dialects.

Many parts of Emacs are designed around a dichotomous view of files as either source code for a programming language or free form text. Markdown lies somewhere in between these two extremes, and sometimes the best route for implementing new features in Emacs is not obvious. As Markdown Mode and my own understanding of the subtleties of Emacs Lisp grow, I hope that Markdown integration in Emacs can become even faster, more seamless, and more robust.

8.2 Further Reading

To keep up with Markdown Mode news, you can follow my blog at https://jblevins.org/log/ or follow the project on GitHub at https://github.com/jrblevin/markdown-mode/. For Emacs news more generally, there is Planet Emacsen, a feed aggregator at http://planet.emacsen.org/, and Sacha Chua's weekly Emacs News at http://sachachua.com/blog/.

I also highly recommend *Mastering Emacs* by Mickey Petersen for all Emacs users. Few could read this book and not learn *something* new about our favorite text editor. *Mastering Emacs* was a primary source of inspiration for me in writing this *Guide*. It is available at https://masteringemacs.org/.

There are also active Emacs communities on the EmacsWiki at https://www.emacswiki.org/, the Emacs StackExchange at https://emacs.stackexchange.com, and on Reddit at https://www.reddit.com/r/emacs/.

Finally, every Emacs user should practice getting help from within Emacs itself, which is often the most detailed and up to date source and certainly the most convenient. A few of the most useful commands are C-h k (describe-key), C-h m (describe-mode), C-h f (describe-function), and C-h v (describe-variable), and C-h a (apropos-command).

Printed in Great Britain
by Amazon